DEAD BODY REPORTED

10 TIPS FOR WINNING A GAME!

70

KT-430-221

GHOSTED: WHAT TO DO WHEN YOU DIE

62

Task Completed!

Published 2021
Little Brother Books Ltd, Ground Floor, 23 Southernhay
East, Exeter, Devon, EX1 1QL
Printed in Poland. ul. Połczyńska 99,01303 Warszawa

books@littlebrotherbooks.co.uk
www.littlebrotherbooks.co.uk

Contributions from: Simon Brew, Claire Brunton,
James Hunt, John Moore, Laura Pelham, Rachel Storry,
Isabel Brew, Thomas Brew

LittleBrother
BOOKS

THE STORY OF AMONG US!

How did Among Us become such an epic game? Here's its history…!

ORIGINALLY ON ANDROID AND IOS

Hard to believe, but many gamers didn't find out about Among Us until the year 2020, when it became hugely popular as lots of people started playing and sharing their games. But Among Us was actually released years earlier on 15th June 2018. It just took a little while to gain momentum! Originally, Among Us was a game for Android and iOS devices (phones and tablets, basically!), but a version for Windows PCs followed five months later. Trouble is, not many people played it at first, and its developer, Innersloth – based in America – nearly gave up. Thankfully, the company stuck with it, and we can now enjoy the game on Nintendo Switch as well.

NOW AVAILABLE ON SWITCH

SPARK!

So who came up with the idea for Among Us? Well, that honour partly belongs to Marcus Bromander, an artist, animator and programmer who was 27 years old when he decided to make the game in 2017.

Since he was a child, Marcus had played Mafia, a social deduction game enjoyed in real life rather than on a computer. Also known as Werewolf, Mafia had been created in 1986 by Dimitry Davidoff, a student at Moscow State University. Lots of other people had adapted it as a fun board game over the following years.

Marcus felt Mafia would also work well as a videogame. He was not the first person to realise this by any means, but he believed he could expand on the game's rules and allow players to do more than make accusations about who was a traitor.

He also knew he needed to keep things simple to make it easy for anyone to understand how to play it. By choosing to use 2D graphics and setting the game in space, he was sure it would be appealing and exciting to all.

As such, a small team got working on it. They took eight months to make the first version and, shortly after the game went on sale, the team noticed how enthusiastic the players were about it. This spurred them on to keep developing it, adding extra tasks and online multiplayer.

After the release of the Windows version, they also included cross-platform play (meaning people on different formats could still play together). Two extra maps were made in 2019, adding a space station and planet base to the original spaceship. There are now four locations in total. Which is your favourite?

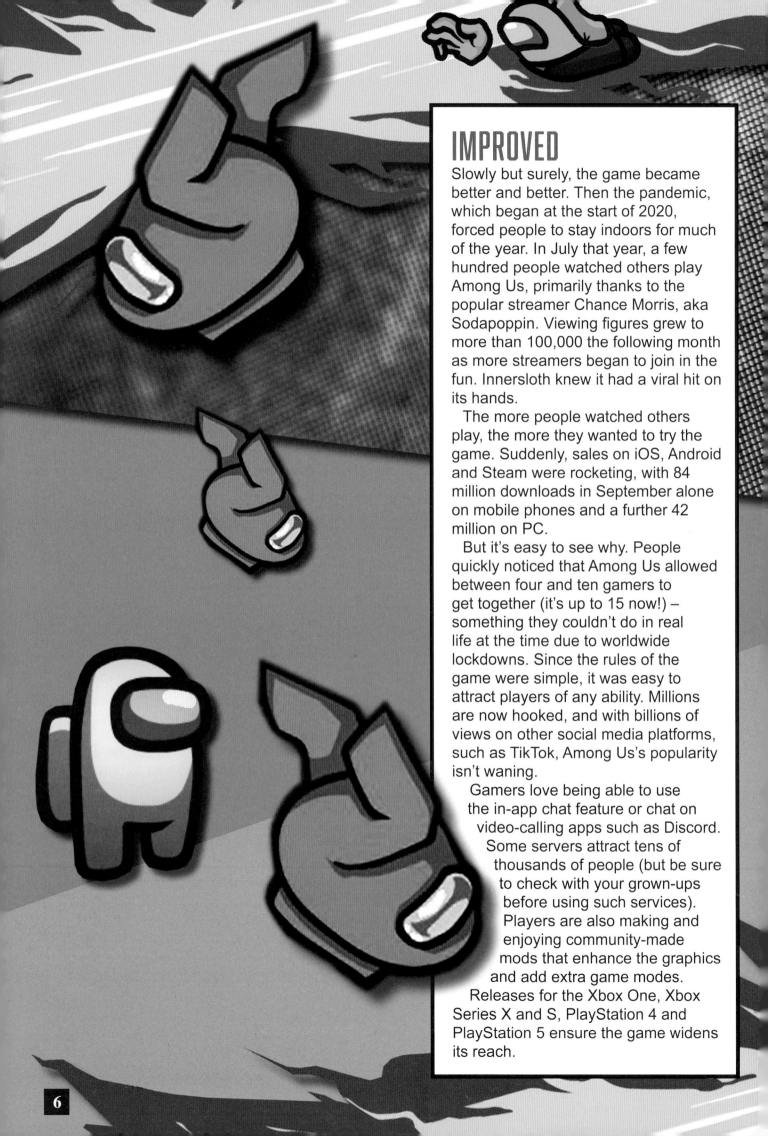

IMPROVED

Slowly but surely, the game became better and better. Then the pandemic, which began at the start of 2020, forced people to stay indoors for much of the year. In July that year, a few hundred people watched others play Among Us, primarily thanks to the popular streamer Chance Morris, aka Sodapoppin. Viewing figures grew to more than 100,000 the following month as more streamers began to join in the fun. Innersloth knew it had a viral hit on its hands.

The more people watched others play, the more they wanted to try the game. Suddenly, sales on iOS, Android and Steam were rocketing, with 84 million downloads in September alone on mobile phones and a further 42 million on PC.

But it's easy to see why. People quickly noticed that Among Us allowed between four and ten gamers to get together (it's up to 15 now!) – something they couldn't do in real life at the time due to worldwide lockdowns. Since the rules of the game were simple, it was easy to attract players of any ability. Millions are now hooked, and with billions of views on other social media platforms, such as TikTok, Among Us's popularity isn't waning.

Gamers love being able to use the in-app chat feature or chat on video-calling apps such as Discord. Some servers attract tens of thousands of people (but be sure to check with your grown-ups before using such services). Players are also making and enjoying community-made mods that enhance the graphics and add extra game modes. Releases for the Xbox One, Xbox Series X and S, PlayStation 4 and PlayStation 5 ensure the game widens its reach.

FUTURE

So what's next? Well, Innersloth had considered making a sequel, but it changed its mind about the idea soon after Among Us 2 was announced. There won't be a sequel now. Instead, the developer is going to continue developing the original game. Its future looks secure, and not at all sus!

ITS POPULARITY ISN'T WANING

AMONG US

Can you believe these amazing numerical facts about Among Us?!?

IN NUMBERS

2018

The year Among Us was first released

60 MILLION

The number of people playing the game every day by the end of 2020!

518 MILLION

The number of Among Us players in June 2021

SHHHHHHH!

13 BILLION

The number of TikTok Among Us video views in October 2020 alone!

15 The number of players who can now

MORE THAN 350 MILLION

The number of copies of Among Us that have been downloaded

57.69%

The number of times the Impostors win the game, according to the official Among Us social media account

THE SKELD MAP GUIDE

The Skeld is the oldest map, set on a starship hurtling through outer space!

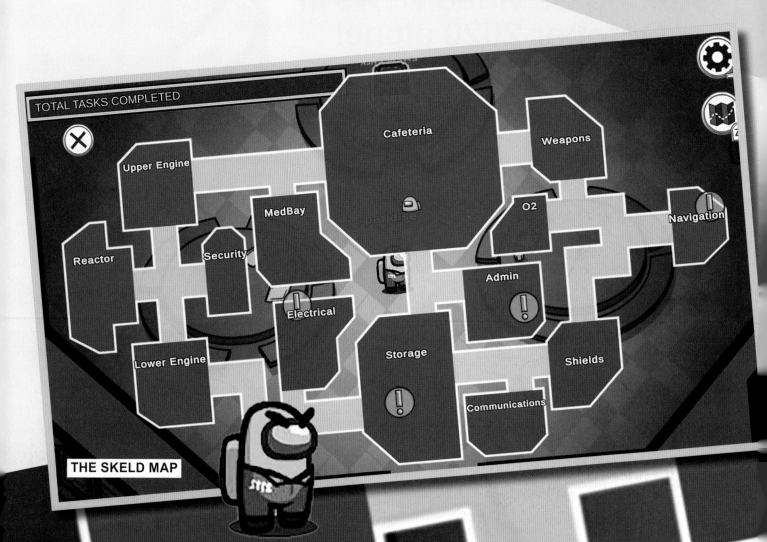

TOTAL TASKS COMPLETED

Upper Engine
Cafeteria
Weapons
MedBay
O2
Navigation
Reactor
Security
Admin
Electrical
Lower Engine
Storage
Shields
Communications

THE SKELD MAP

paridise

Storage

MEDBAY

L Submit Scan
L Inspect Sample

NAVIGATION

S Chart Course
S Stabilise Steering
S Download Data
S Accept Diverted Power
C Fix Wiring

O2

S Clean O2 Filter
S Accept Diverted Power
L Empty Chute

REACTOR

S Unlock Manifolds
L Start Reactor

SECURITY

S Accept Diverted Power
C Fix Wiring

SHIELDS

S Accept Diverted Power
S Prime Shields

STORAGE

L Fuel Engines
L Empty Garbage
L Empty Chute
C Fix Wiring

UPPER ENGINE

S Accept Diverted Power
L Fuel Engines
L Align Engine Output

WEAPONS

S Download Data
S Accept Diverted Power
L Clear Asteroids

TASK KEY

S – Short
L – Long
C – Common

VENT GROUPS

Admin / Cafeteria / Shields
Hallway
Electrical / MedBay / Security
Navigation / Weapons
Weapons / Shields
Lower Engine / Reactor
Reactor / Upper Engine

ADMIN

S Upload Data
C Fix Wiring
C Swipe Card

CAFETERIA

S Fix Wiring
L Empty Garbage
C Download Data

COMMUNICATIONS

S Download Data
S Accept Diverted Power

ELECTRICAL

S Calibrate Distributor
S Divert Power
S Clean Vent
S Download Data
C Fix Wiring

LOWER ENGINE

S Accept Diverted Power
L Fuel Engines
L Align Engine Output

paridise

REACTOR   SECURITY

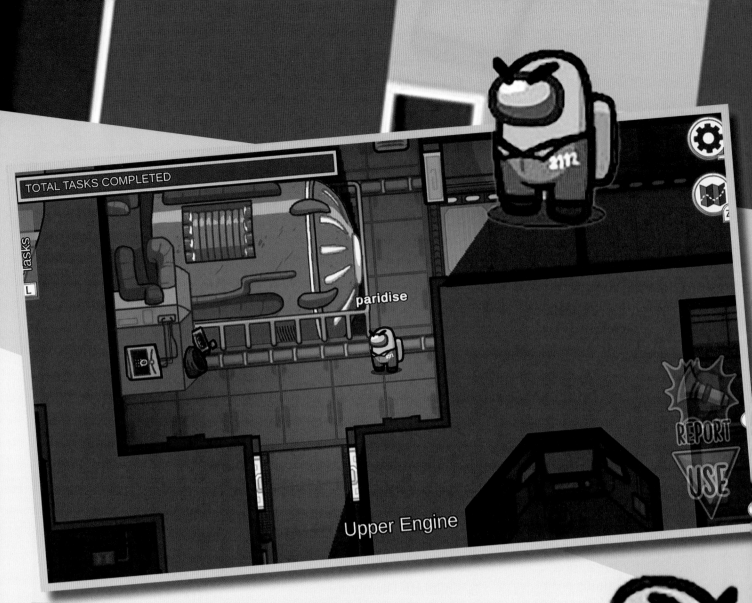

paridise

Upper Engine

REPORT

USE

THE SKELD TIPS & TRICKS

Imposters can sabotage the doors in the Lower Engines, Medbay, Security and Storage, causing them to close automatically for 10 seconds. Most of these rooms contain vents, allowing the imposter to escape afterwards.

The only rooms on this map without any vent access are O2, Communications and Storage.

If you have no hat and no name label, there is a floating box in Storage that you can disappear behind completely. This is useful for hiding from imposters AND lying in wait for crewmates.

The corridors leading to Security, Navigation, Admin and MedBay contain security cameras.

Electrical is a dangerous spot as many of the tasks are located right next to a vent.

Sabotaging in the O2 room begins the Oxygen Depleted event, which can be fixed by entering codes in Admin and O2.

The Light sabotage can be both triggered and fixed in Electrical.

The Comms sabotage can be triggered and fixed in Communications.

The Reactor Meltdown event is triggered and fixed in the Reactor – two people must scan their fingerprints simultaneously to disable it.

THE SKELD FACTS & TRIVIA

The Skeld is the second smallest map in the game, and the only one with tasks in every named location. In fact, every location has at least two tasks, so you'll get to know the map very well!

The name of the map, "Skeld", is Swedish for "shield". This is also the name of the spaceship you're on, which was presumably given this name because it is shaped like a shield!

The Skeld is the only map where the spawn point AND meeting place is the same location – in this case, the Cafeteria.

Four visual tasks occur in The Skeld that allow players to easily prove their innocence when visual tasks are enabled. It has the most visual tasks of any map in the game: Clear Asteroids (Weapons), Submit Scan (Medbay), Prime Shields (Shields) and Empty Garbage & Empty Chute (Storage).

On April Fool's day, the map is flipped horizontally, becoming ehT dlekS. You can also set the date on your device to October 31st to see Halloween decorations.

On the Nintendo Switch edition, controllers with rumble enabled will start to shudder as you get closer to the engines.

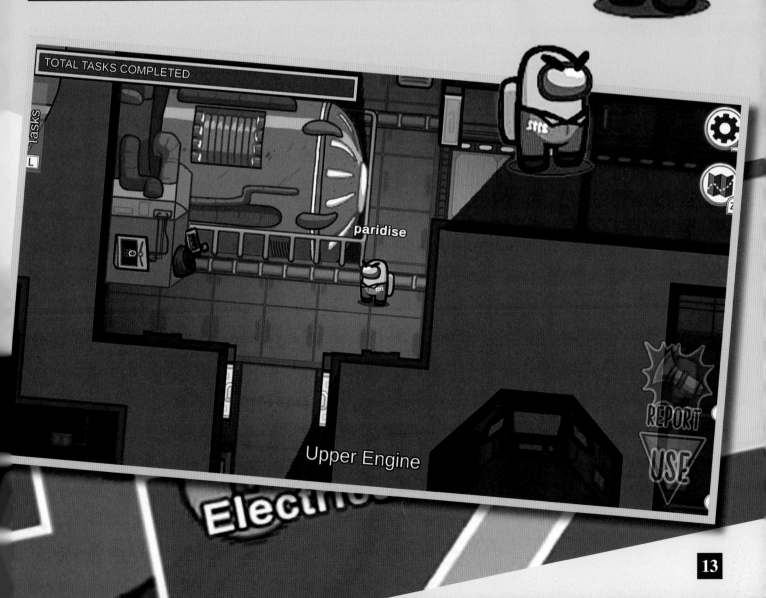

TOTAL TASKS COMPLETED

paridise

Upper Engine

Electric

CUSTOMISE YOUR AVATAR

How to give yourself a distinct look in Among Us!

COLOR

HAT

Within Among Us, you can customise your avatar with different colours and accessories. Not only does it mean you can make yourself look more fun, but it also helps with playing the game. Accessories make the players more recognisable, meaning the Imposter can be easier to spot – or harder to get away with!

HOW TO

When you enter a game lobby, head to the laptop in the top left corner and click CUSTOMIZE. Here, you can change four settings: COLOR, HAT, PET, SKIN.

COLOR

This is the colour you'll wear in the game. You can set it to your favourite, but if you enter a different game and someone else is already wearing that colour, the game will change yours automatically to a colour not in use.

CUSTOMISE YOUR AVATAR

Quickmask

START
1/15

CUSTOMIZE

On the main page, head to the $ sign in the bottom right corner.

Here, you'll see different options to buy. Themed outfit bundles for each location, as well as different hats, pets and skins. Each option has a name and price. You can see what it looks like on and the cost in the left-side pane. Time to get creative!

HAT

Time to accessorise! There are various different options to make your avatar stand out. This will stay the same for all games unless you change it yourself.

PET

This is where any pets you buy will show up. These will also stay the same for all games unless you change them. There are no free pets, so you need to buy them from the shop for any to appear. Make sure you check with your grown-up before spending any money, though!

SKIN

A full outfit already designed, like pets, these are only available from the shop. Any you purchase will show up here afterwards for you to wear.

| Color | Hat | Pet | Skin | Game |

TRY ON HATS

PET

SKIN

21.6.30o

CHECK THE PRICE

Restore Purchases

AIRSHIP

Cyborg RHM

£1.99

MIRA HQ
MAP GUIDE

MIRA HQ is a skyscraper research facility and the headquarters for the company, MIRA

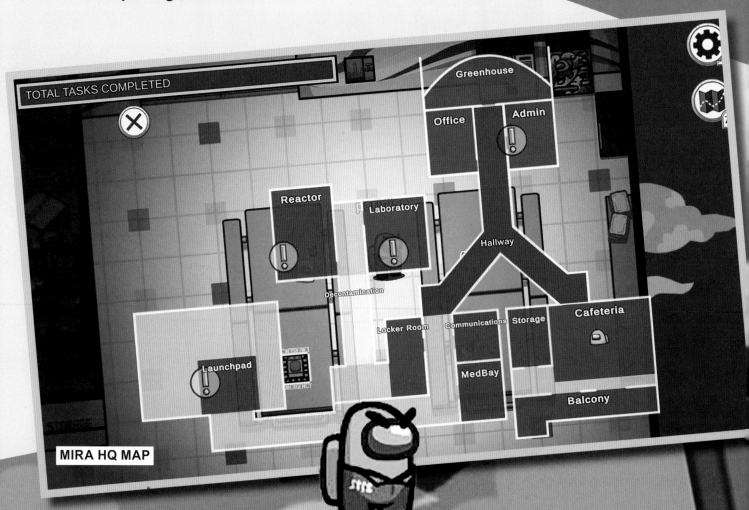

TOTAL TASKS COMPLETED

Greenhouse

Office   Admin

Reactor   Laboratory

Hallway

Decontamination

Locker Room   Communications   Storage   Cafeteria

Launchpad

MedBay

Balcony

MIRA HQ MAP

Greenhouse

C Fix Wiring

LAUNCHPAD

S Fuel Engines
S Run Diagnostics
L Accept Diverted Power

LOCKER ROOM

C Fix Wiring

MEDBAY

L Submit Scan
L Inspect Sample

OFFICE

S Process Data
L Accept Diverted Power

REACTOR

S Unlock Manifolds
S Divert Power
L Start Reactor

STORAGE

C Fix Wiring
L Water Plants

TASK KEY

S – Short
L – Long
C – Common

VENT GROUPS

Launchpad / Reactor / Locker Room / Medbay / Balcony / Admin / Office / Greenhouse / Hallway / Laboratory / Decontamination

ADMIN

S Prime Shields
S Chart Course
C Accept Diverted Power
L Enter ID Code

BALCONY

L Clear Asteroids
S Measure Weather

CAFETERIA

S Buy Beverage
S Empty Garbage
L Accept Diverted Power

COMMUNICATIONS

L Accept Diverted Power

DECONTAMINATION

No Task

GREENHOUSE

S Clean O2 Filter
L Water Plants
L Accept Diverted Power
C Fix Wiring

HALLWAY

C Fix Wiring

LABORATORY

S Sort Samples
S Assemble Artifact
S Accept Diverted Power

TOTAL TASKS COMPLETED

tasks

L

paridise

Balcony

REPORT

USE

MIRA HQ TIPS & TRICKS

MIRA HQ has the most efficient vent system, as all the vents are connected in a single group, making them especially useful for imposters to travel around in. If you're spotted venting, a good trick is to vent straight to the Cafeteria and call a meeting before you can be accused!

In the Communications room, it is possible to access the Doorlog ability, which marks all players who pass through the Hallway. There are three sensors: blue at the top (between Office and Admin), green on the left (by  Communications) and red on the right (by the Cafeteria).

Imposters can trigger the Oxygen Depleted sabotage from the Greenhouse. To undo it, any player can enter the reset codes in the PIN pads in the Greenhouse and the Hallway next to the Medbay. Both pin codes must be entered to fix the sabotage.

The Light Sabotage can be both triggered and fixed in the Office. The Comms sabotage is triggered in Communications, but must be fixed by entering codes in the Office and Comms rooms.

If you have no hat and no name label, you can hide completely behind the Satellite dish in the Balcony.

MIRA HQ is the second map to be added to the game, and the smallest with just 14 locations.

Players spawn on the Launchpad, but emergency meetings are held in the Cafeteria.

It is the only map with no security cameras or Door Sabotage ability, but it compensates for this by being the only one with Doorlogs.

You can set the date on your device to October 31st to see Halloween decorations.

MIRA HQ is set on the 111th floor of a skyscraper. Notably, the data you upload from other maps are processed here, as evidenced by the tasks lists in this map.

MIRA HQ has only one visual task: the Submit Scan task in the MedBay.

The windows in the Laboratory are one-way glass, meaning players can see into the room from the outside, but anyone inside can't see out.

The Reactor Meltdown sabotage is dangerous on this map, because players must frequently pass through Decontamination to reach the Reactor, losing precious seconds. For this reason, a meltdown takes 15 seconds longer to occur on this map.

PUZZLES

LOCKS AND KEYS

Put your Among Us talents to use with this pair of challenges!

PUZZLE 1:
Which of these keys is the odd one out?

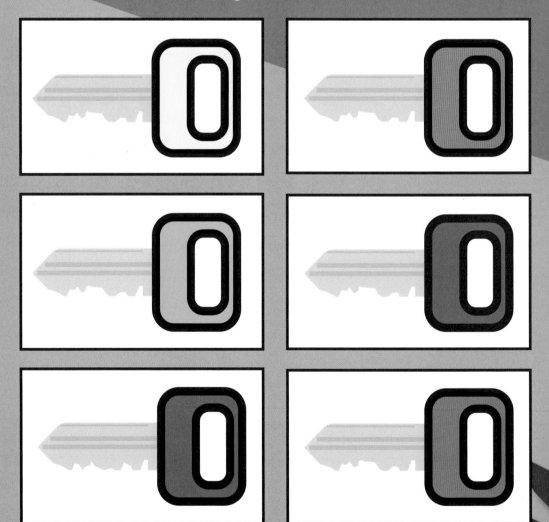

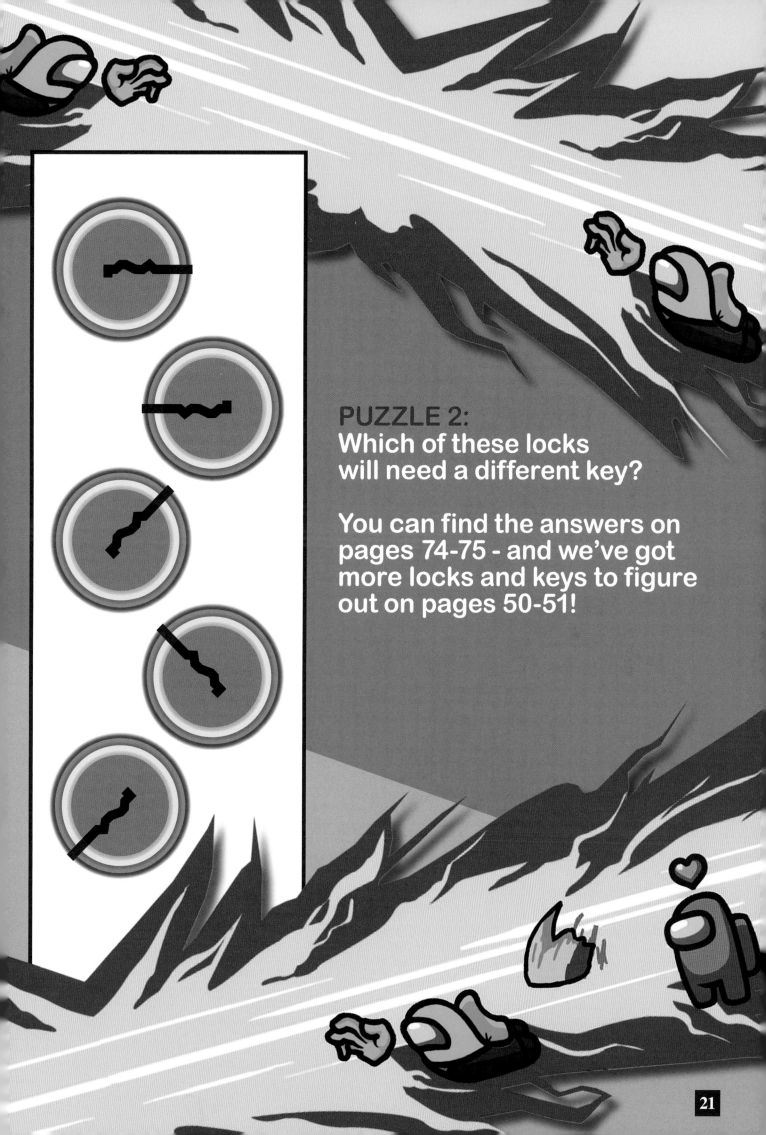

PUZZLE 2:
Which of these locks
will need a different key?

You can find the answers on
pages 74-75 - and we've got
more locks and keys to figure
out on pages 50-51!

POLUS MAP GUIDE

Polus is a research outpost on the planet Polus, where the crew hide out, unaware they're being stalked...

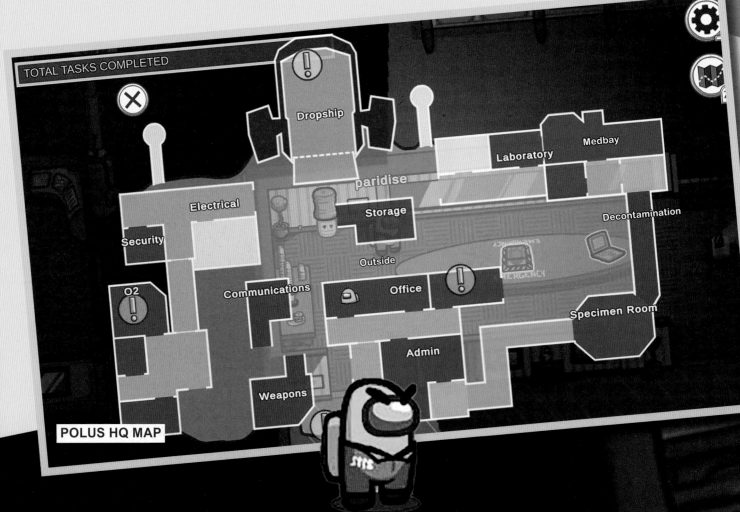

TOTAL TASKS COMPLETED

Dropship

paridise

Medbay

Laboratory

Electrical

Storage

Decontamination

Security

Outside

Specimen Room

O2

Communications

Office

Admin

Weapons

POLUS HQ MAP

TOTAL TASKS COMPLETED

Dropship: Insert Keys
Boiler Room: Open Waterways (0/3)
Node_CA: Fix Weather Node (0/2)
Laboratory: Record Temperature

paridise
EMERGENCY

Office

REPORT
USE

TASK KEY

S – Short
L – Long
C – Common

VENT GROUPS

Outside (Laboratory) /
Outside (Electrical)
Electrical / Outside / O2
Laboratory / Admin / Outside
Outside / Office Hallway /
Storage

ADMIN

No tasks

COMMUNICATIONS

L Reboot Wifi
L Upload Data

DECONTAMINATION

C Fix Wiring

DROPSHIP

S Chart Course
C Insert Keys

ELECTRICAL

C Fix Wiring
L Download Data

LABORATORY

S Fix Weather Node
S Record Temperature
S Repair Drill
S Align Telescope
C Fix Wiring (right)
C Fix Wiring (left)

MEDBAY

S Submit Scan
L Inspect Sample

O2

S Empty Garbage
S Monitor Tree
S Fill Canisters
L Download Data
C Fix Wiring

OFFICE

L Download Data
L Replace Water Jug
C Scan Boarding Pass
C Swipe Card
C Fix Wiring

OUTSIDE

S Record Temperature
L Fix Weather Node
L Fuel Engines
L Open Waterways

SECURITY

No Tasks

SPECIMEN ROOM

S Store Artifacts
S Unlock Manifolds
L Download Data
L Start Reactor

STORAGE

L Fuel Engines

WEAPONS

S Clear Asteroids
L Download Data

TOTAL TASKS COMPLETED

Tasks

paridise

Dropship

REPORT
USE

23

Tasks

paridise

O2

REPORT

USE

POLUS TIPS AND TRICKS

On Polus, the security viewscreen only displays one location at a time, so you have to cycle through the four locations to view them all. The cameras have a larger view, though, so you can see more.

The security camera areas are located in the bottom left of the map, to the right of Electrical, to the top right of Storage, between Office and Communications, to the right of the Office and between Weapons and Admin.

The doors in Polus can all be sabotaged individually with no cool-down between them. However, to reopen a sabotaged door, players only need to press all four buttons.

Although players are thrown into the lava when ejected, you can't walk into the lava by accident. Phew!

Imposters can sabotage the seismic stabilisers in the Outside area. Two stabilisers in the northwest and northeast of the map must be reset to fix the sabotage. You can also sabotage Comms (in Communications) and Lights (in Electrical).

Every player is given a different key slot, so you can spot an imposter if they use the same key slot as another player.

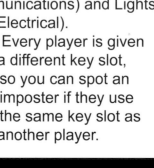

POLUS FACTS & TRIVIA

Dropship is the spawn location for this map, and is also used as the lobby for multiplayer games.

After a meeting is called, players will be spawned in the Office.

Polus was the third map to be added to the game and is the second largest of the four currently available.

It is the only map with unique-looking vents. Here, they appear as holes in the ground rather than the standard metal grates.

The visual tasks for Polus are Clear Asteroids (Weapons) and Submit Scan (MedBay).

A vital signs machine in the Office shows the status of every player's life signs – anything red means they've died but not been reported.

Although Polus has an O2 room, you can't sabotage the oxygen.

On this map, if an imposter kills a crewmate while watching security, the body will be stashed behind the camera area.

The Specimen Room can only be accessed by going through Decontamination. There are no vents or other doors in and out.

TOTAL TASKS COMPLETED

Tasks

L

paridise

REPORT

USE

AMONG US JOKES!

Take a break and enjoy a quick giggle!

WHY DOES THE IMPOSTER KEEP GETTING ANGRY IN AMONG US?

Because they keep needing to vent!

SHHHHHH!

WHAT DO YOU CALL THE ODD ONE OUT IN A BAG OF AMONG US SPAGHETTI?

The im-pasta!

HOW ARE AMONG US PLAYERS TRANSPORTED AROUND?

On the Sus Bus!

SHHHHHHH!

HOW DID THE DETECTIVE WORK OUT WHO THE IMPOSTER WAS IN AMONG US?

They sussed it out!

DID YOU HEAR ABOUT THE AMONG US PARTY?

It was a real killer!

WHY DID AMONG US DO BADLY WHEN IT WENT ON REALITY TV?

It was voted off!

WHY DID THE AMONG US MAP BOOK FALL APART?

Nothing Skeld it together!

WHERE WOULD YOU STORE A COPY OF AMONG US?

In a spare space!

SHHHHHHH!

AIRSHIP MAP GUIDE

The biggest and newest map, the Airship is a safe haven from MIRA and the only place not owned by them!

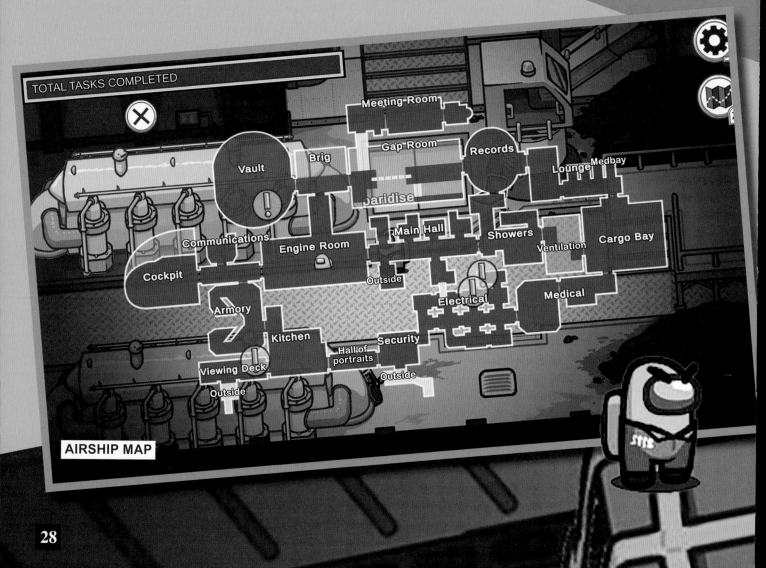

TOTAL TASKS COMPLETED

Meeting-Room

Gap-Room

Records

Lounge Medbay

Vault

Brig

Paridise

Communications

Main Hall

Showers

Ventilation

Cargo Bay

Engine Room

Cockpit

Outside

Electrical

Medical

Armory

Kitchen

Security

Viewing Deck

Hall of portraits

Outside

Outside

AIRSHIP MAP

28

Hall of Portraits

TASK KEY

S – Short
L – Long
C – Common

VENT GROUPS

Vault / Cockpit / Viewing Deck
Engine Room / Kitchen / Main Hall
Main Hall / Gap Room / Gap Room
Showers / Records / Cargo Bay

ARMORY

S Put Away Rifles
S Put Away Pistols
S Accept Diverted Power
S Download Data

BRIG

S Upload Data

CARGO BAY

S Download Data
L Fuel Engines
L Unlock Safe
C Fix Wiring

COCKPIT

S Accept Diverted Power
S Stabilise Steering
L Upload Data

COMMUNICATIONS

S Download Data

ELECTRICAL

S Calibrate Distributor
S Divert Power
L Reset Breakers

ENGINE ROOM

S Accept Diverted Power
L Fuel Engines
C Fix Wiring

GAP ROOM OUTSIDE

L Upload Data

RECORDS

S Download Data
S Sort Records

SECURITY

L Rewind Tape

SHOWERS

S Accept Diverted Power
S Fix Shower
S Pick Up Towels
L Empty Garbage
C Fix Wiring

VAULT

S Download Data
S Polish Ruby
S Dress Mannequin

VENTILATION

L Start Fans

VIEWING DECK

S Upload Data
C Fix Wiring

Security

TOTAL TASKS COMPLETED

Tasks

L

TANK BOX

paridise

Cargo Bay

REPORT

USE

AIRSHIP TIPS AND TRICKS

In the Airship, Electrical is made up of small, interconnected rooms with randomly opening doors. However, the doors will eventually open in a way that allows all rooms to be accessed.

Imposters can't directly sabotage the doors in the Vault, though they can sabotage the Brig doors, which is the only exit.

The Avert Crash Course sabotage can be caused in the Gap Room and resolved using the keypads on either side of the Gap Room. This takes 90 seconds, which is longer than any other sabotage in the game.

The main hall has restricted vision, as the lighting inside is low. Any players outside the hall can't see what is happening inside.

Ventilation contains a gap that can't be crossed. You can access the left side of the room from the Showers and the right side of the room from the Cargo Bay. However, imposters can cross the gap quickly using vents in the Showers and Cargo Bay!

The Airship's cameras are located in the Vault, Records, Cargo Bay, Security and the Meeting Room.

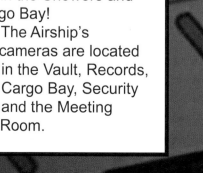

AIRSHIP FACTS & TRIVIA

The Airship is the most recent map to be added to the game at the time of writing. It is the largest, the only one with moving platforms and ladders, and it features 20 different locations!

The Airship is the only map that doesn't have any visual tasks, so you can't use the ability to detect imposters. For that reason and its general size and complexity, it's probably one of the hardest maps to win on!

You're able to select the respawn location from a list of six after choosing an emergency meeting: Engine Room, Records, Main Hall, Kitchen, Cargo Bay and Meeting Room.

You can fix sabotaged lights in Electrical, but the lights can be sabotaged from the Gap Room, Viewing Deck or Cargo Bay.

The Admin ability for this map is in the Cockpit rather than Admin!

The Hall of Portraits has the longest name of any location in Among Us.

The Gap Room is called the Gap Room because it must be crossed using the floating platforms.

This map is a reference to the game Fleeing the Complex, which was also developed by InnerSloth, the creators of Among Us.

PUZZLES

Test your Among Us knowledge and skills!

WORDSEARCH

Can you sus out and find these Among Us terms hiding in our word - search? It'll take all your sleuthing skills! Answers are on pages 74-75...

Cafeteria

Boiler Room

Communications

Cargo Bay

Balcony

Decontamination

Hall of Portraits

Kitchen

Laboratory

Locker Room

Med Bay

MIRA HQ

Navigation

Polus

Security

Shields

The airship

The Skeld

Weapons

Upper Engine

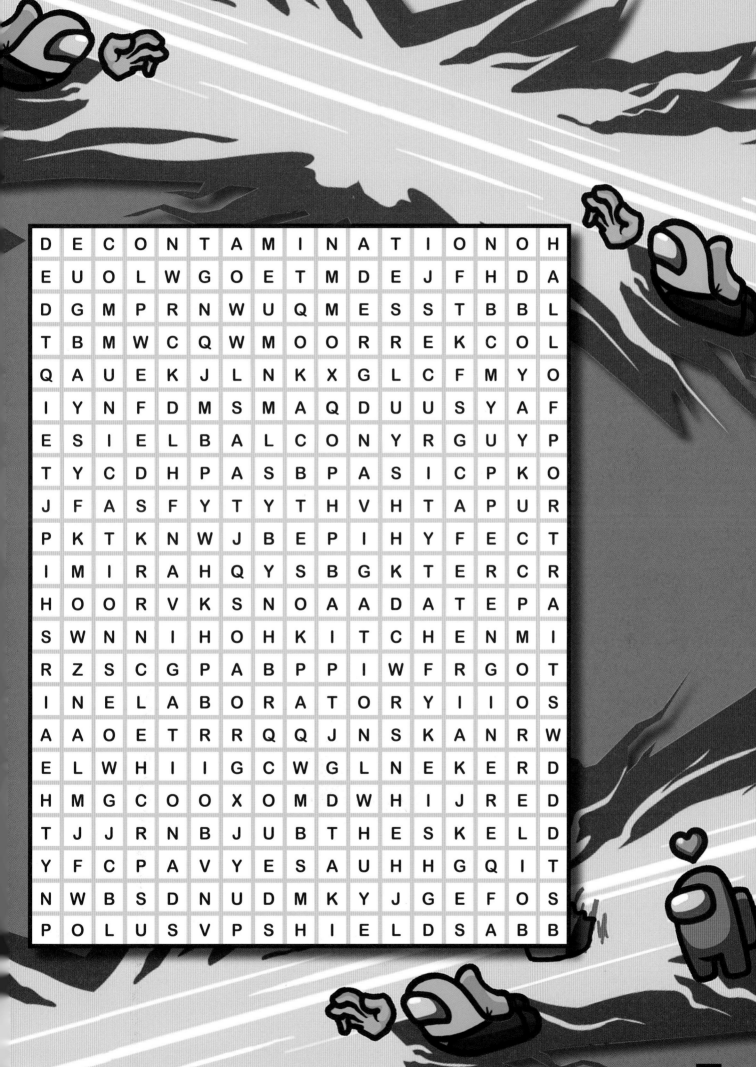

SPOTTING
WHO'S SUS

Figuring out which players are sus and which aren't is the key to winning Among Us. Here are our expert tips…

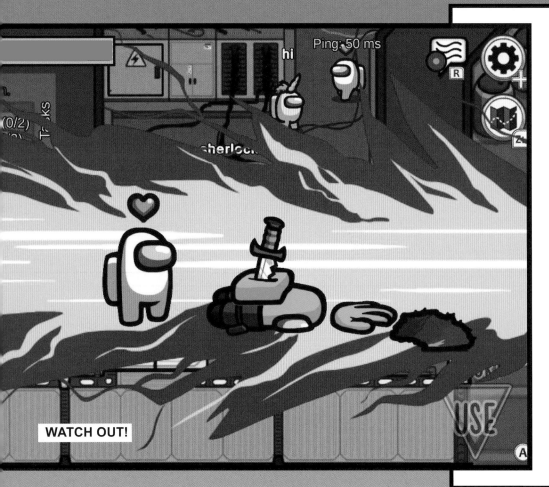

WATCH OUT!

WATCH OUT!

The number one tip – the thing you should always be doing – is taking an opportunity to spy on the other players. You can do this by looking at their position on the map and seeing whether they're mysteriously at the scene of a murder without reporting it. Or you can directly witness them in the act of sabotage using the security cameras. But this is basic stuff and you probably already know it. What else can you do to track down the most suspicious crewmates around?

WATCH THE TASKS

This one's surprisingly simple as the taskbar tells you what actions your crewmates have done. So if you watch someone walk up to a panel, then leave without having completed an action, there's a good chance they're trying to look busy while they plot their next kill. Don't immediately accuse them, of course. Just keep an eye on their name and see if they actually complete any tasks. The longer it goes without you seeing them do anything, the more chance they're the one sewing chaos.

WHO'S TRAVELLING TOO FAST?

Imposters have the advantage when it comes to travelling around the map as they can use the vents. If you see a player coming out of a vent or going right into one, there's no question that they're an imposter. However, what if they're travelling distances too quickly? If you see someone apparently teleport across the map, or you follow them into a room only to see they've disappeared, there's a good chance they're using vents. As soon as you know they've done this, it's time to report them.

FOLLOW PAIRS AROUND

Imposters usually take the opportunity to kill when there's no one else around. So if you see two people go into a room with one exit and only one player come out, there's a good chance they just took out their supposed friend in private. Likewise, if someone closes the door manually on their way in, they might be trying to get some privacy to commit evil deeds.

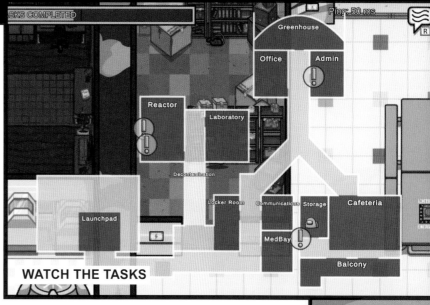

WATCH THE TASKS

WHO'S TRAVELLING TOO FAST?

FOLLOW PAIRS AROUND

As soon as you can, check for a body or see if they've vented, assuming you don't find a player standing there, looking confused but alive. It will tell you all you need to know.

WHO ISN'T HELPING?

One thing you should remember about imposters is that they don't have any tasks to complete. So if they're unable to get a player on their own to take them out, there's very little they can do except hang around. If you spot a crewmate wasting time or watching a large group until someone they can follow heads out of the room, it's because they've been stalking their prey! Anyone who's a legit crewmate will be completing their tasks and not just lying in wait.

WHO ISN'T HELPING?

WHO ALWAYS TRAVELS SOLO?

Unlike legitimate crewmates, imposters don't have to worry about being murdered when they travel on their own. So if you see someone running off like they haven't got a care in the world, it might be because they don't! The smartest crewmates know to always travel in pairs (at least!) whenever possible. If someone keeps going off independently, it might be because they don't have to worry as THEY'RE the person doing the takedowns. Don't put too much stock in this one on its own, though, as you might just be playing with a newbie who doesn't realise travelling solo is practically signing their own death warrant!

WHO ALWAYS TRAVELS SOLO?

WHAT TO IGNORE

TRUST YOUR GUT

Ultimately, the best way to tell whether someone is sus or not is to listen to your gut. Are they acting weird, but you can't explain how? Did they ignore a corpse in the same room as them? Are they constantly accusing random people? All of these things might add up to let you know that someone is trying to find ways to deflect suspicion. Short of being killed by the imposter or catching them in the act, there are very few ways to say for sure who's sus. Trust your instincts!

WHAT TO IGNORE

There are plenty of ways to find out who the imposter is, but which things aren't a lot of help?

Reporting a body Imposters might self-report to throw you off the scent, but it's equally likely that someone genuinely found and reported it. There's no way of knowing whether it's a self-report or not.

Fixing a sabotage Again, imposters can both cause AND fix sabotages, so seeing someone fix a problem doesn't mean they're necessarily on your team.

Accusing an imposter If there are multiple imposters, they all know who's the imposter and who isn't. To survive longer, someone might throw their evil cohorts under a bus by accusing them and taking the heat off themselves!

Ping: 50 ms

paridise

eenhouse

AMONG US IN MINECRAFT

**Do you like Among Us AND Minecraft? Who doesn't!?
Here's how you can combine the two!**

AMONG US MULTIPLAYER

If you have the Java Edition of Minecraft, there are a number of dedicated Among Us servers, where you can play a version of the game built entirely in a Minecraft world. Handed the role of crewman or imposter, you perform tasks in full 3D versions of the Among Us maps against other real players. Getting started doesn't require any additional mods or downloads, just the Java Edition of the game (sorry, Bedrock players!).

Two popular servers are:
Mineville: play.mineville.org (look for "imposter")
Performium: amongus.performium.net (look for "Amongoose")
Remember to get permission from your grown-up before playing online!

AMONG US MAPS

Alternatively, if you just want to play on the maps, so you can explore the Among Us world with complete freedom, as if it really existed, there are tonnes of downloadable creations that recreate the locations found

ange 6821

fiHum4n

AMONG US MULTIPLAYER

in the game. Again, Java Edition players can check out the Among Us Map tag on Planet Minecraft for all sorts of downloadable treats: **www.planetminecraft. com/projects/tag/ amongusmap/** Remember, these maps don't have the gameplay of Among Us; they're just recreations of the locations!

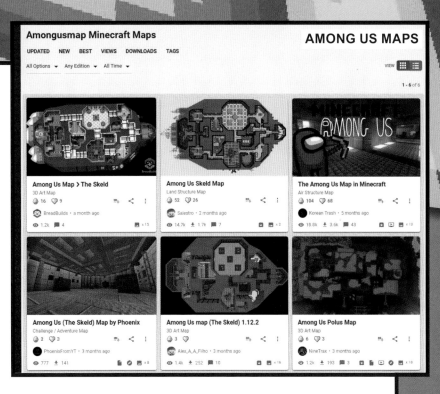

AMONG US PARKOUR

Want to play an Among Us map that isn't just a recreation of stuff from the game? We've got just the choice for you: an Among Us-themed parkour map! This too is a Java Edition-exclusive, which does at least mean it's free to download and play. There are eight checkpoints as you leap your way around a precarious course designed to test your skill at both parkour and Minecraft in general. It's available now from the location below – just visit it and click "download Minecraft map", then unzip the file into your Minecraft saves to play it.

www.minecraftmaps.com/parkour-maps/among-us-parkour

BEDROCK EDITION CONTENT

Thanks for sticking with us, Bedrock Edition players! Sadly, we aren't aware of any Among Us servers that you can play on, but the good news is you have the entire Minecraft shop to get content from. We liked the look of the "AMONG SUS" (you read that correctly) pack, which contains over 20 Among Us-style skins for the price

of just 490 minecoins. Map-wise, look out for AMONG IMPOSTERS by The Craft Stars, which also costs 490 minecoins and contains another 20 skins, plus an Among Us-style map to test them out in. You should be able to get these on consoles, mobile devices and tablets, and the Windows 10 Edition. Enjoy!

AMONG US PARKOUR

BEDROCK EDITION CONTENT

CUSTOM GAME IDEAS

Discover new ways to play Among Us with this selection of mini-games

As well as the standard game of Among Us, players all over the world have been coming up with their own mini-games or mods to play within the game. Some of these games require downloading custom content, but here are a few that only need changing the in-game settings and a bit of pre-planning with your friends.

When playing these mini-games, the most important thing is to remember to play in a private lobby with friends, not a public one with strangers. Otherwise, the other players won't know which rules you're using!

COPS & ROBBERS

» The imposter is the Cop, and all crewmates are Robbers.

» Designate one room as the holding cell – this stays the same for the whole game.

» The Cop must count down, allowing for all the Robbers to hide. Robbers cannot start their tasks until the countdown has ended.

» When a Robber is caught, they must follow the Cop to the holding cell. Here, they can be killed. Make sure you have set a long cooldown time for the kills.

» Robbers waiting for execution can be rescued by other crewmates, but only one at a time, and must return to a designated 'safe spot' before they can complete tasks again.

» Robbers win if they complete all the tasks before death, and the Cop wins if they successfully execute all Robbers first.

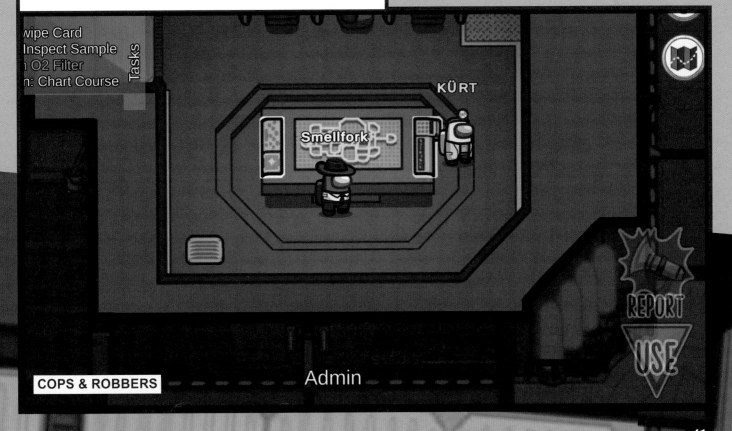

Wipe Card
Inspect Sample
O2 Filter
n: Chart Course

Tasks

KÜRT

Smellfork

REPORT

USE

Admin

HIDE AND SEEK

» In the lobby, give crewmates the maximum viewing setting and the Imposter the minimum. Make sure you only have one Imposter.

» The Imposter must reveal themselves at the start and then countdown, just like in normal hide and seek.

» The minute the Imposter starts to count, crewmates should run. They need to balance completing their tasks with hiding from the known Imposter.

» When the Imposter gets to zero, they can start hunting down crewmates – and no need to avoid looking sus!

» Crewmates shouldn't report dead bodies as the Imposter is known.

» When dead, you must mute your mic; you cannot help fellow players verbally, though you can continue your tasks.

CAN YOU WIN?!

Victory

QUIT

PLAY AGAIN

TOTAL TASKS COMPLETED

Ping: 50 ms

Shields: Prime Shields
O2: Clean O2 Filter
Electrical: Divert Power to Security (0/2)

Tasks

Smellfork

THE GAUNTLET

THE GAUNTLET

» The same mission objectives as the main game, but it's a one-on-one battle and relay race between one crewmate and one Imposter at a time.

» Make sure to have more than one Imposter!

» Decide before you start if you want to allow sabotage – locking doors and damaging the oxygen supply is not recommended.

» Imposters and crewmates must each pick their first player. When chosen, the crewmate is released first to finish all their tasks.

» After a small countdown of your choice (around 15 seconds), the chosen Imposter is also released to hunt them down.

» If the Imposter kills the crewmate, return to the spawn area for the next Imposter and crewmate to go.

» If the crewmate completes all of their tasks, they should call an emergency meeting and everyone votes out that Imposter.

» Repeat until either all tasks are completed, or all crewmates are dead.

NO MEETINGS

» Make sure to have only one Imposter at a time.

» All players should play the game as normal, aiming to complete tasks and avoid being murdered.

» The Imposter must stay secret and can sabotage as they wish, just like in a regular game.

» Dead bodies cannot be reported, and no meetings can be called. The only way to win is to complete all tasks or kill all crewmates.

» Players can talk throughout the game until they are murdered; at this point, they must mute themselves to keep the Imposter identity hidden.

These are just some of the mini-games out there to play, but there are even more being created daily!

HOW TO AVOID BEING CAUGHT

The number one objective of any imposter: how to hide!

DO: SELF-REPORT

A self-report is when an imposter kills someone, then calls a meeting to say that they've found a body. This is a risky move because you could place yourself at the crime scene by the process of elimination. But it's also a way to potentially throw people off your scent because you can claim you found the body and throw suspicion on someone else. Self-reporting is an expected move, so just be ready for someone to accuse you of it and have a response prepared if they ask what you were doing in that room...

DO SELF REPORT

EMERGENCY MEETING

DO: MAKE SURE YOUR KILLS ARE CLEAN

A clean kill takes place in a room where no one else can see you, and you can escape without being spotted. Don't kill players in communal spaces, and use vents to hide in if you're worried that someone else might be close. The quicker you can get away, though, the better, and keep in mind that security cameras might be watching, even if players aren't! If your kill isn't clean and someone sees you, try to turn suspicion on them as quickly as possible!

DO MAKE SURE YOUR KILLS ARE CLEAN

DON'T: VOTE TOO QUICKLY

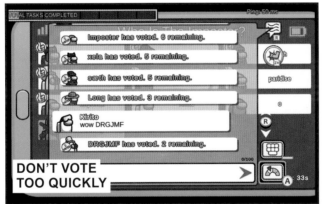

DON'T VOTE TOO QUICKLY

Unless you've called a meeting because you outright witnessed a murder, there's no reason anyone should vote before any discussion has been had. That means when someone who hasn't called a meeting votes straight away, they're usually an imposter trying to hide their own guilt. When you're the imposter, wait calmly until a discussion has been had before voting. As long as suspicion doesn't fall on you, it's fine to take your time in picking who to vote for. If anything, it's probably better to do it that way!

DON'T: VENT TOO OFTEN

Vents are super-useful for hiding in and for getting around the map quickly. However, only imposters can use them, which makes them an easy way to get caught! Save venting for when you're sure no one else is around and that you're not being followed. If you disappear in a room seconds after entering it, players will know you used a vent. They can be hard to resist because of how convenient (and fun!) they are, but every time you vent you increase the chance of getting found out – it's that simple.

DON'T VENT TOO OFTEN

HOW TO BE A GOOD CREW

To win the game, you have to complete every task – here's how to do your bit!

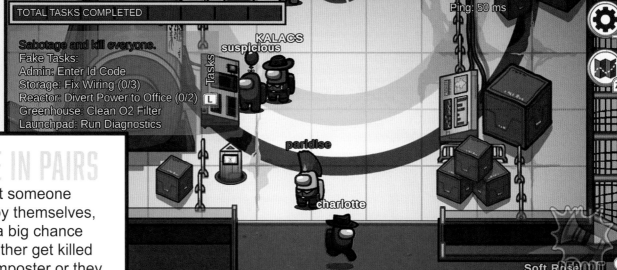

TOTAL TASKS COMPLETED

Ping: 50 ms

Sabotage and kill everyone.
Fake Tasks:
Admin: Enter Id Code
Storage: Fix Wiring (0/3)
Reactor: Divert Power to Office (0/2)
Greenhouse: Clean O2 Filter
Launchpad: Run Diagnostics

Tasks

KALACS
suspicious

paridise

charlotte

Soft Rose

MOVE IN PAIRS

Launchpad

K8L

SABOTAGE

REPORT

MOVE IN PAIRS

If you let someone run off by themselves, there's a big chance they'll either get killed by the imposter or they ARE the imposter. Moving in pairs makes it harder for the imposter to achieve their goals because everyone's always watching someone else! If there are multiple imposters, it also means you'll never be outnumbered by them – but watch out for two imposters pairing together!

ALWAYS TRY TO FIX SABOTAGES

It doesn't matter where you are; when a sabotage is revealed, you should always head towards it, even if you're the furthest person from it! You'll instantly lose if you don't get it fixed, and imposters will try to pick off people while they're distracted. So the more players who try to repair the sabotage, the better. Your survival depends on it!

MATE

WATCH OUT FOR COMMON TASKS

Some tasks, like swiping a keycard on Polus, are given to everyone. So if you don't have it, no one else does, and if you see someone "completing" that task in front of you, they're an imposter who's just pretending. Keep your eyes peeled and report it to your crewmates!

DON'T WASTE YOUR MEETINGS

Rather than spending meetings trying to accuse an imposter, encourage people to organise. Visual tasks are those where onlookers can see the results (e.g. a Medbay scan). If you've got one, invite players to watch so they can rule you out as the imposter. You can also organise people into pairs or gather evidence. Don't try to convince anyone else until you're sure who's an imposter.

DON'T SPAM

Repeating stuff helps no one. In meetings, keep your statements simple and clear. The more you talk, the more people are likely to miss what others say. Likewise, if you call a meeting, make sure you've got some factual information to share that can't wait. The more meetings you call, the less time you have to complete the tasks and investigate!

SKIP VOTING IF YOU'RE UNSURE

If you don't know who the imposter is – and early on, you probably won't – don't just vote for whoever gets accused first. It's in crewmates' interests to keep as many people around until they know who's an imposter, so acting on a flimsy accusation is just doing the imposter's job for them! You can abstain from the vote, and remember to tell people that's what you're doing!

ALWAYS TRY TO FIX SABOTAGES

PRETEND YOU'RE AN IMPOSTER

SHHHH

Whether as a survival strategy or just an attempt to throw some chaos into the game, here's how you can draw people's suspicion!

WHY PRETEND?

You might wonder why you'd want to pretend to be the imposter, but there are a few good reasons.

For example, if you ARE the imposter, sometimes a double-bluff is the way to stay in the game: the more you claim to be the imposter, the more suspicious it will be. People will think you're just trying to confuse them and go for someone else. After all, who would want to make it obvious that they're the imposter?! Likewise, if you're not the imposter, being very clear about making people think you are would be

WHY PRETEND?

DEAD BODY REPORTED

a surefire way to get people to leave you alone for the same reason – because why would anyone say that if it was true?

ACCUSE EVERYONE ELSE

Imposters are most likely to accuse other people of being the imposter, so when you get the chance, make sure you come out guns blazing! Accuse others quickly and often, make up details, say anything you can to get suspicion to fall on others – maybe even

SHHHHHHH!

two or three times in one meeting. It will baffle everyone, and they'll probably just ignore what you're saying, leaving you safe to survive another round.

SAY YOU'RE THE IMPOSTER

When all else fails, you could always just take the craziest route and TELL people you're the imposter. There's a good chance they won't believe you because why would you give that information away unless you were trying to mess with them? This isn't always going to work and could backfire if there are no other viable choices – but hey, anything's worth a try, right? This strategy could work best over multiple rounds with the same player because if you say it every time, then they won't know when to believe you! Confused? They will be!

ACT SHIFTY

If you want to draw people's attention, make yourself look like an imposter. Hang around vents, run off by yourself, and pretend to do tasks instead of actually doing them, especially if it's a common task that others haven't been assigned. It will draw suspicion whether that's correct or not! The goal is to look as obvious as possible, so the blame falls on you, and whether that's just for fun or as a strategy to confuse others, it's worth knowing how!

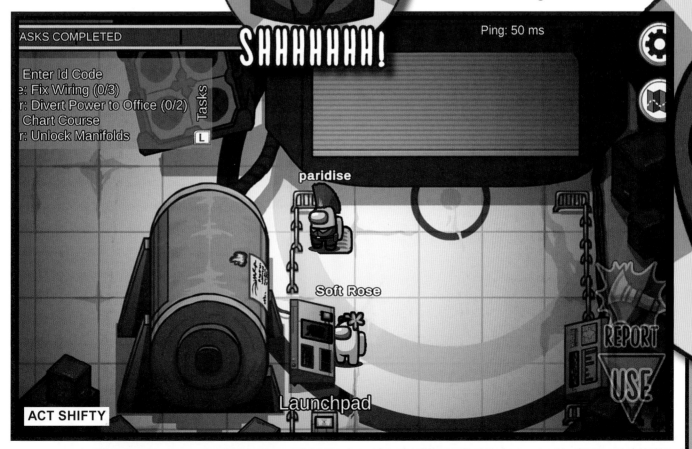

PUZZLES

Test your Among Us knowledge and skills!

You're going to need all your Among Us talents to unlock our mini-games here!

PUZZLE 1:
Which of these keys is the odd one out?

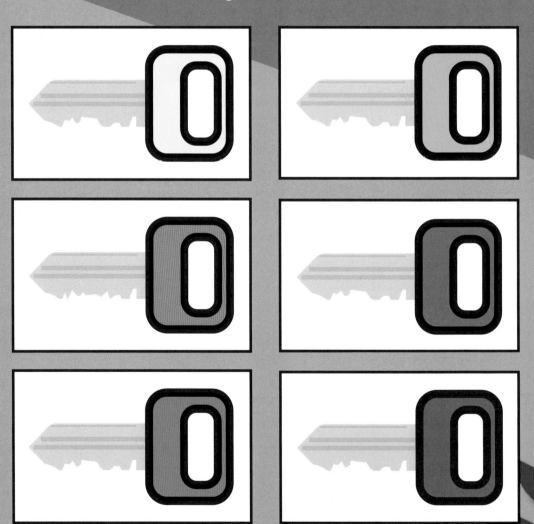

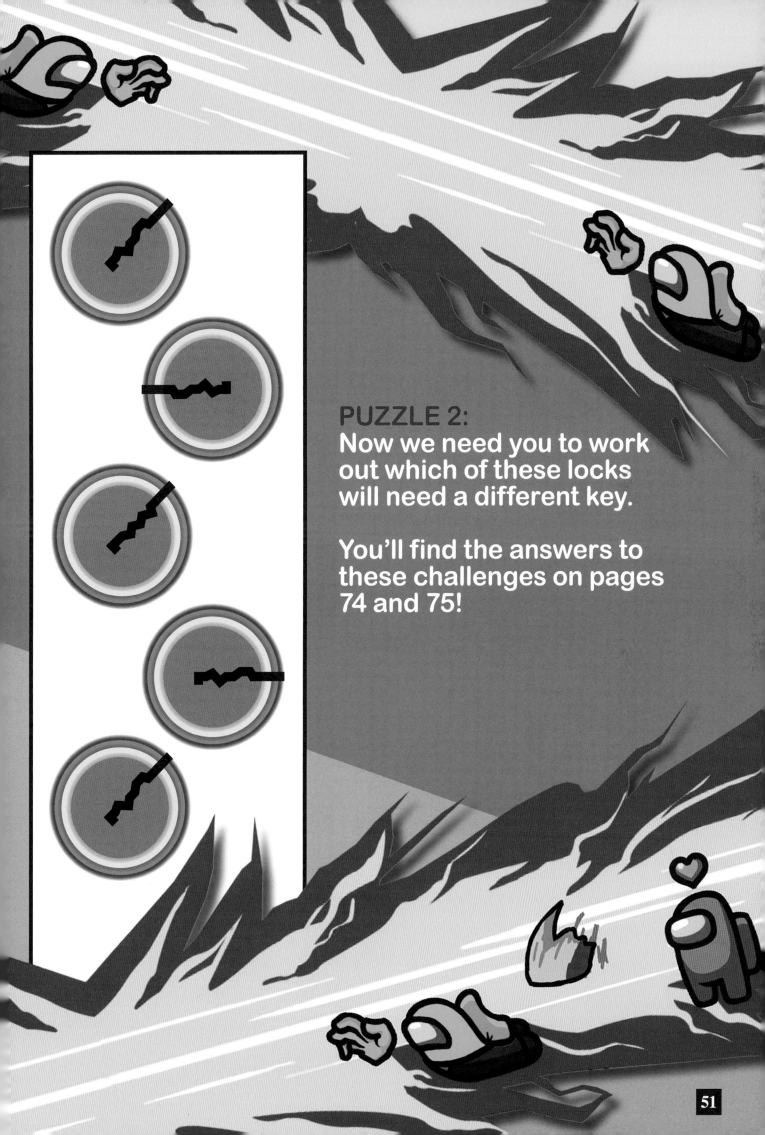

PUZZLE 2:
Now we need you to work out which of these locks will need a different key.

You'll find the answers to these challenges on pages 74 and 75!

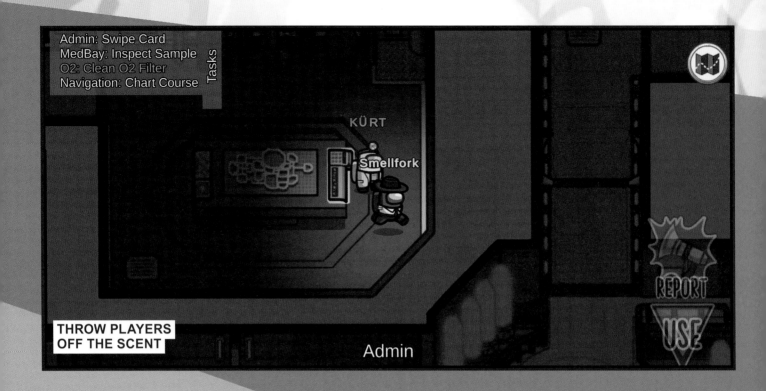

KÜRT

Smellfork

REPORT

USE

**THROW PLAYERS
OFF THE SCENT**

Admin

f you're the Impostor, you have a few tricks to throw other players off the scent – and one of them is using the sabotage options that the game provides you with. Used properly, they can be the difference between winning and losing! You probably know the basics already: if you're playing as the Impostor, you can tap on the sabotage button, and a map will pop up of the current level. Some of the sabotages – if the crewmates don't get to them in time – will lead to victory for the Impostors! The oxygen, for instance, is really rather important, so if they don't fix it before the clock runs down, it's game over and another win for the Impostors!

SABOTAGE
ESSENTIALS

When playing as the Impostor, sabotaging can make the difference between winning and losing!

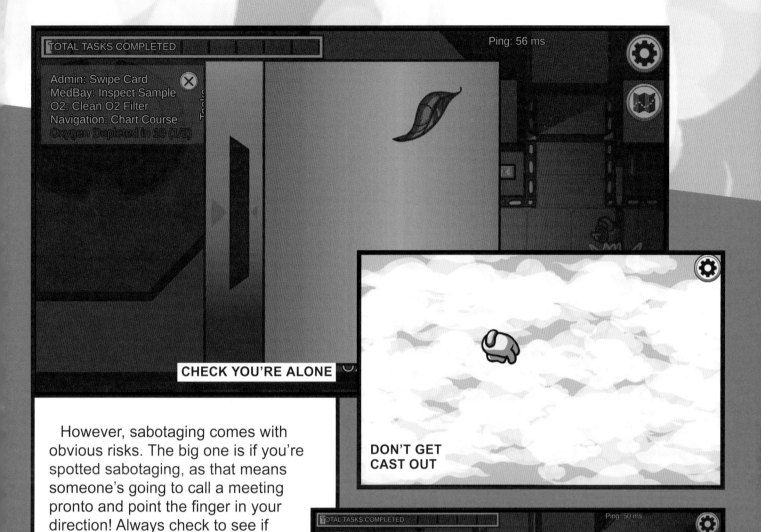

TOTAL TASKS COMPLETED

Admin: Swipe Card
MedBay: Inspect Sample
O2: Clean O2 Filter
Navigation: Chart Course
Oxygen Depleted in 10 (1/2)

Ping: 56 ms

CHECK YOU'RE ALONE

DON'T GET CAST OUT

However, sabotaging comes with obvious risks. The big one is if you're spotted sabotaging, as that means someone's going to call a meeting pronto and point the finger in your direction! Always check to see if you're alone before sabotaging. If something goes wrong in a certain place on the deck, and someone else knows you're the only person there, they're going to get sus very, very quickly!

MORE TIPS

One of the problems for an Impostor is usually, crewmates tend to move together in a block. It's a good way for them to stay safe. However, if you're the Impostor and looking to get an advantage, why not sabotage the lights and quickly move in for a kill? It gives you a couple of seconds, so you need to move quickly. You could even walk around with the main group of crewmates to try and blend in!

One less useful thing is if you're killed and become an Impostor ghost. You'll still be able to do some sabotaging, but, arguably, there's not much point in doing so.

TOTAL TASKS COMPLETED

Admin: Swipe Card
Storage: Fix Wiring (0/3)
Reactor: Start Reactor
Cafeteria: Empty Garbage (0/2)
Electrical: Download Data (0/2)
Electrical: Divert Power to Upper Engine (0/2)
Navigation: Stabilize Steering
Navigation: Chart Course
Upper Engine: Clean Vent
Oxygen Depleted in 10 (1/2)

Ping: 50 ms

Smellfork

FIX WHAT YOU'VE SABOTAGED

ONE MORE THING

Just because you can sabotage, it doesn't mean that you always should. Choose your sabotages carefully, and remember that every time you undertake one, you're leaving yourself a little more open to being discovered. The correctly timed sabotage really can swing a game in your favour – or leave you cast out into space!

If you really want to throw other players off the scent, be seen fixing what you've sabotaged! Then they're more likely to think that you're on their side than trying to kill them.

USING CAMERAS

You can give yourself an upper hand by heading to Security...

CAMERAS CAN BE HELPFUL

f you head into the Security room on an Among Us map, you'll have access to the security cameras in the game. Given that ordinarily you can't see too much when you're walking around a deck, these can be a brilliant way to get the upper hand!

Lots of players don't make much use of the cameras, and of course there's a risk if you're stood there looking at the screen and the impostor comes up behind you. As always, one of the main tips with Among Us is to stay alert – you never know who is around the corner!

However, don't dismiss the idea of using the cameras because they can give you an edge.

But what should you be looking for? Well, if you're one of the crew, keep an eye on the vents when looking at the camera footage. If you see someone disappearing behind a vent, you know you've caught one of the impostors (although you've still got to convince everybody else, of course). One additional tip here: whilst a camera doesn't show you everything, if someone goes into a room and doesn't come out for a long time, there's a good chance they've used a vent.

Furthermore, when you see a crewmate who appears to be standing still, that usually means they're completing a task, which in turn suggests they're not the impostor. Of course, that's not always the case, but it's a good rule of thumb. Not for nothing is the Security room one of the most popular places for an Among Us kill!

Don't overlook the fact that using the cameras can alert you to where a dead body is a little bit quicker. You still have to make your way there to report it, which is made extra scary by the fact that you know the killer can't be too far away. But again, Among Us is a game where it pays to get crucial information quickly.

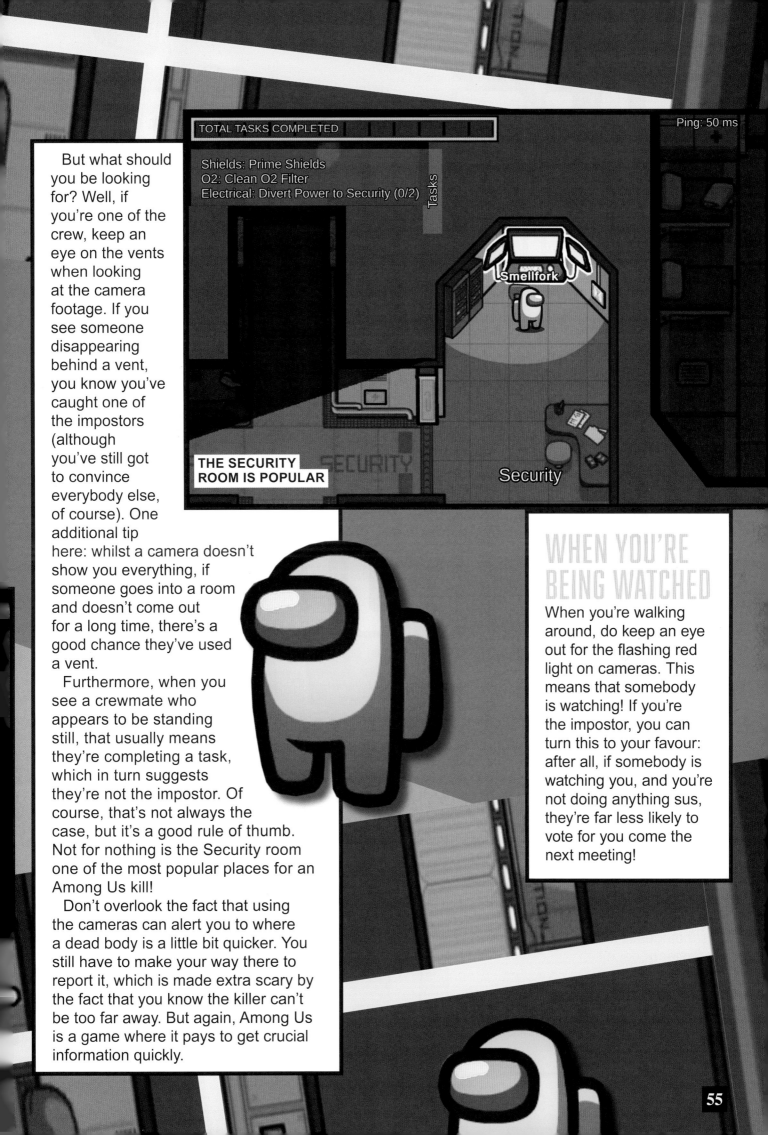

TOTAL TASKS COMPLETED

Ping: 50 ms

Shields: Prime Shields
O2: Clean O2 Filter
Electrical: Divert Power to Security (0/2)

Tasks

Smellfork

THE SECURITY ROOM IS POPULAR

SECURITY

Security

WHEN YOU'RE BEING WATCHED

When you're walking around, do keep an eye out for the flashing red light on cameras. This means that somebody is watching! If you're the impostor, you can turn this to your favour: after all, if somebody is watching you, and you're not doing anything sus, they're far less likely to vote for you come the next meeting!

THE BEST AMONG US YOUTUBERS

We round up some of the most entertaining Among Us streamers out there!

#Myth #AmongUs
My FASTEST Impostor Wins in Among Us...

Name: Myth
Subscribers: 4.61M
Nationality: American
Streaming since: 2013

Why are they great?
Watching Myth trick his crewmates and chuckle away as he kills and sabotages is hilarious. He is the master of deceit.

What else do they play & stream?
Myth is a big Warzone player, but he also plays Fortnite, Rainbox Six: Siege and Rust.

Myth
4.61m subscribers

HOME   VIDEOS   PLAYLISTS   COMMUNITY   CHANNELS   ABOUT

Uploads   ▶ PLAY ALL

Day One 21 Bomb - MY WARZONE GRIND BEGINS
22K views • 1 day ago

900IQ KAY/O FLASHES Ft. Pokimane, Sydeon &...
43K views • 2 weeks ago

BLOODHUNT - A NEW Battle Royale! (Exclusive...
109K views • 2 weeks ago

MYTH'S FIGHT CLUB #2 TEAM ANDROID vs...
31K views • 1 month ago

Name: **Ninja**
Subscribers: 24.1M
Nationality: American
Streaming since: 2011

Why are they great?
He's great at interrogating his crewmates and edits his gameplay excellently so the tension really builds.

What else do they play & stream?
Ninja plays a tonne of games including Fortnite, Apex Legends and Call of Duty Blackout.

Ninja ✓
24.1M subscribers

HOME   VIDEOS   PLAYLISTS   COMMUNITY   STORE   CHANNELS   ABOUT

SUBSCRIBE

I HAVE A FORTNITE SKIN!!! #ninjaskin

I HAVE A FORTNITE SKIN!!! #ninjaskin
16,796,322 views · 1 year ago

Get The OFFICIAL NINJA SKIN starting Thursday 6 p.m. CST-Sunday 7 p.m in the Fortnite store

SUBSCRIBE HERE to never miss a video!
http://bit.ly/SubscribeNinja
Join my Notification Squad by clicking the 🔔 Bell
WATCH ME LIVE ON MIXER https://mixer.com/ninja

Fake Tasks:
Admin: Swipe Card
Electrical: Fix Wiring (0/3)
Weapons: Clear Asteroids (0/20)
Cafeteria: Download Data (0/2)
Weapons (0/2)

3:31 / 14:45   MedBay

#TeamNinja #Ninja #AmongUs
10,000 IQ PLAY TO TRICK ALL OF THEM!! - AMONG US!

Twitch

SUBSCRIBE

o-Karts w/
amlinz (Old...
month ago

Name: **SSundee**
Subscribers: 18M
Nationality: American
Streaming since: 2009

Why are they great?
Funny, enthusiastic and always yelling, SSundee does brilliant playthroughs on all the newest mods. He's a great teamplayer as well as a convincing and clever imposter – it's almost impossible not to laugh.

What else do they play & stream?
SSundee plays Minecraft and Fortnite as well as various other random games.

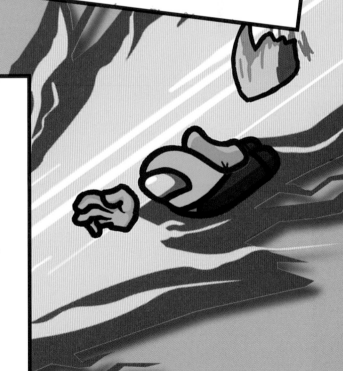

POKIMANE

@POKIMANELOL YOUTUBE.COM/POKIMANE
@POKIMANELOL FACEBOOK.COM/POKIMANE
DOWNLOAD CASH APP

Pokimane ✓
6.65M subscribers

SUBSCRIBE

HOME | VIDEOS | PLAYLISTS | COMMUNITY | CHANNELS | ABOUT

Pokimane's 2021 ROOM TOUR + Gaming Setup!
1,138,023 views • 1 week ago

Welcome to my 2021 Room Tour! I show you guys my gaming area which includes my setup and stream backgrounds with all of my art and collectables + my bedroom area which has both of my closets, my vanity and bathroom :)

Name: Pokimane
Subscribers: 6.65M
Nationality: American
Streaming since: 2014

Why are they great?
Pokimane is really fun, sweet and enthusiastic. She plays normal Among Us as well as modded games where she and her friends take on new roles.

What else do they play & stream?
As well as playing Fortnite, Pokimane does Vlogs, reaction videos and Q&As.

Who Is The Impostor?

#Pokimane #AmongUs #TheAirship
i exposed the impostor in 5 SECONDS with this secret trick - NEW AIRSHIP MAP
428,178 views • Apr 7, 2021
23K 383

Victory

#disgsuiedtoast #among... ...TOAST big brain duo...
why you can't fo...
1,057,369 views •   51K 466 CLIP SHARE SAVE

Name: Disguised Toast
Subscribers: 3.53M
Nationality: Canadian
Streaming since: 2015

Why are they great?
Disguised Toast spent eight months doing only Among Us content, making him an expert on the game with tonnes of amazing videos.

What else do they play & stream?
Most of his recent content is Among Us, but he does have older videos on games like Hearthstone.

Disguised Toast ✓
3.53M subscribers

DISGUISEDTOAST

HOME | VIDEOS | PLAYLISTS | COMMUNITY | CHANNELS | ABOUT

SUBSCRIBE

The Final Episode - Among Us (20,000 IQ ...

whaddup Baby

The Final Episode - Among Us (20,000 IQ Special)
2,653,504 views • 1 month ago

The day has finally come. Toast's 20,000 IQ Among Us special is here...

Subscribe to Disguised Toast! ► http://bit.ly/1cRxhZa

Watch me on Facebook Gaming! ►
https://fb.gg/DisguisedToast

READ MORE

Name: Sykkuno
Subscribers: 3.53M
Nationality: American
Streaming since: 2011

Why are they great?
His commentary is great, and even though he's not the best Imposter, he's really good at emergency meetings and swaying the vote.

What else do they play & stream?
Sykkuno plays a load of games like Grand Theft Auto 5, Fortnite and Animal Crossing.

Name: Hafu
Subscribers: 306k
Nationality: American
Streaming since: 2015

Why are they great?
Not just making great YouTube videos, she's known as one of the top Among Us players in the world. She's been called trustworthy by others, and her lobbies are usually filled with some of the best and most fun players.

What else do they play & stream?
She is a ranked Hearthstone player as well as playing World of Warcraft and Bloodline Champions.

Sykkuno
2.65M subscribers

HOME   VIDEOS   PLAYLISTS   COMMUNITY   CHANNELS   ABOUT

SUBSCRIBE

THE PERFECT GAME! 1v6 - Among Us ft. Valkyrae, Disguise...
3,202,585 views · 10 months ago

Follow Sykkuno!
Twitch : https://www.twitch.tv/sykkuno
Twitter : https://twitter.com/Sykkuno
Instagram : http://instagram.com/sykkuwu

Friends in this video!
Valkyrae : https://www.youtube.com/channel/UCWxl...

I GOT KICKED OUT THE LOBBY

4:29 / 11:51

THE PERFECT GAME! 1v6 - Among Us ft. Valkyrae, Disguised Toast & friends

121K   1.1K   CLIP   SHARE   SAVE

3,202,585 views · Aug 29, 2020

Name: 5Up
Subscribers: 717k
Nationality: American
Streaming since: 2015

Why are they great?
A dedicated player, they've been grinding away at the game, racking up all kinds of hours. Known for their skill as an Imposter, they've been dedicating themselves to new custom maps recently.

What else do they play & stream?
They have a handful of videos on other games, but 5Up remains dedicated to the art of Among Us.

Name: Wildcat
Subscribers: 7.88M
Nationality: American
Streaming since: 2011

Why are they great?
Rather than providing live commentary as he plays, Wildcat takes his games and provides commentary on them afterwards, adding a great narrative arc to them. His editing skills and music choices make him not just a great player, but a great YouTuber.
Be warned, though, there is swearing in the video commentary from both Wildcat and other players.

What else do they play & stream?
Wildcat, also known as Tyler, plays a whole range of games, including various Pokémon and Call Of Duty games, as well as Minecraft and Spyro.

AMONG US IN ROBLOX

Want to combine Roblox AND Among Us? You're not the first! Here are some ways to mix up your favourite games!

WHY PLAY IN ROBLOX?

We all love the normal version of Among Us, but in Roblox you can play more or less the same game but with a whole bunch of new content and avatar items, with one important difference: it's in full 3D! This is a great way to connect with new fans, allow people who don't own Among Us to get in on the action, and try out different ways of playing the game. The original is still the best, but these versions are fun too!

CREWMATES by Lionly Studios

Crewmates is still in beta, but it's still an excellent version of Among Us, with most of the gameplay already modelled. The 3D world looks just like a recreated version of the Roblox world, and even though it isn't finished, you can have a great time with the basic game as it's played now. There are six badges to collect – can you acquire them all?

WHY PLAY IN ROBLOX?

AMONGST US by Wizard Studios

This one looks a bit more realistic in its art style! Again, it's a recreation of the standard game with several badges to collect, and best of all, the ability to create private servers for free! Check it out!

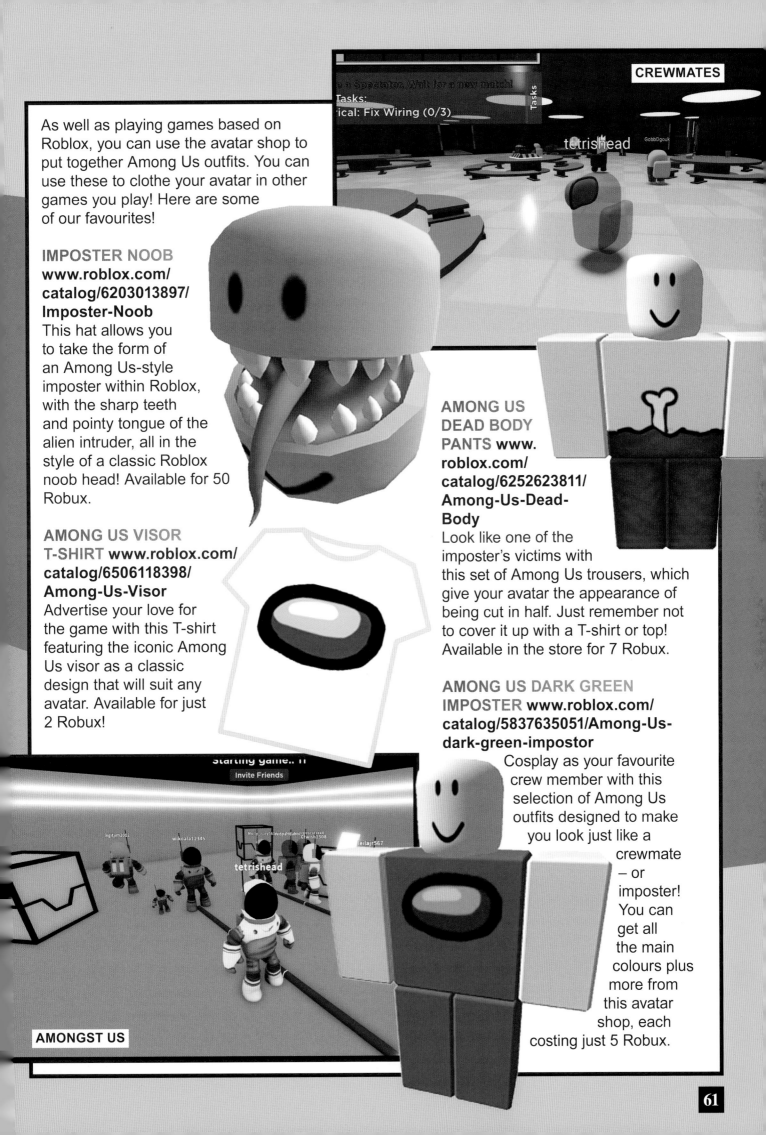

As well as playing games based on Roblox, you can use the avatar shop to put together Among Us outfits. You can use these to clothe your avatar in other games you play! Here are some of our favourites!

IMPOSTER NOOB
www.roblox.com/
catalog/6203013897/
Imposter-Noob

This hat allows you to take the form of an Among Us-style imposter within Roblox, with the sharp teeth and pointy tongue of the alien intruder, all in the style of a classic Roblox noob head! Available for 50 Robux.

AMONG US VISOR
T-SHIRT www.roblox.com/
catalog/6506118398/
Among-Us-Visor

Advertise your love for the game with this T-shirt featuring the iconic Among Us visor as a classic design that will suit any avatar. Available for just 2 Robux!

AMONG US DEAD BODY PANTS www.
roblox.com/
catalog/6252623811/
Among-Us-Dead-
Body

Look like one of the imposter's victims with this set of Among Us trousers, which give your avatar the appearance of being cut in half. Just remember not to cover it up with a T-shirt or top! Available in the store for 7 Robux.

AMONG US DARK GREEN
IMPOSTER www.roblox.com/
catalog/5837635051/Among-Us-
dark-green-impostor

Cosplay as your favourite crew member with this selection of Among Us outfits designed to make you look just like a crewmate – or imposter! You can get all the main colours plus more from this avatar shop, each costing just 5 Robux.

CREWMATES

Tasks:
ical: Fix Wiring (0/3)

tetrishead

GobbDgouk

Starting game.. 1!

Invite Friends

legitjim2012

wikoala12345

tetrishead

leilajr567

AMONGST US

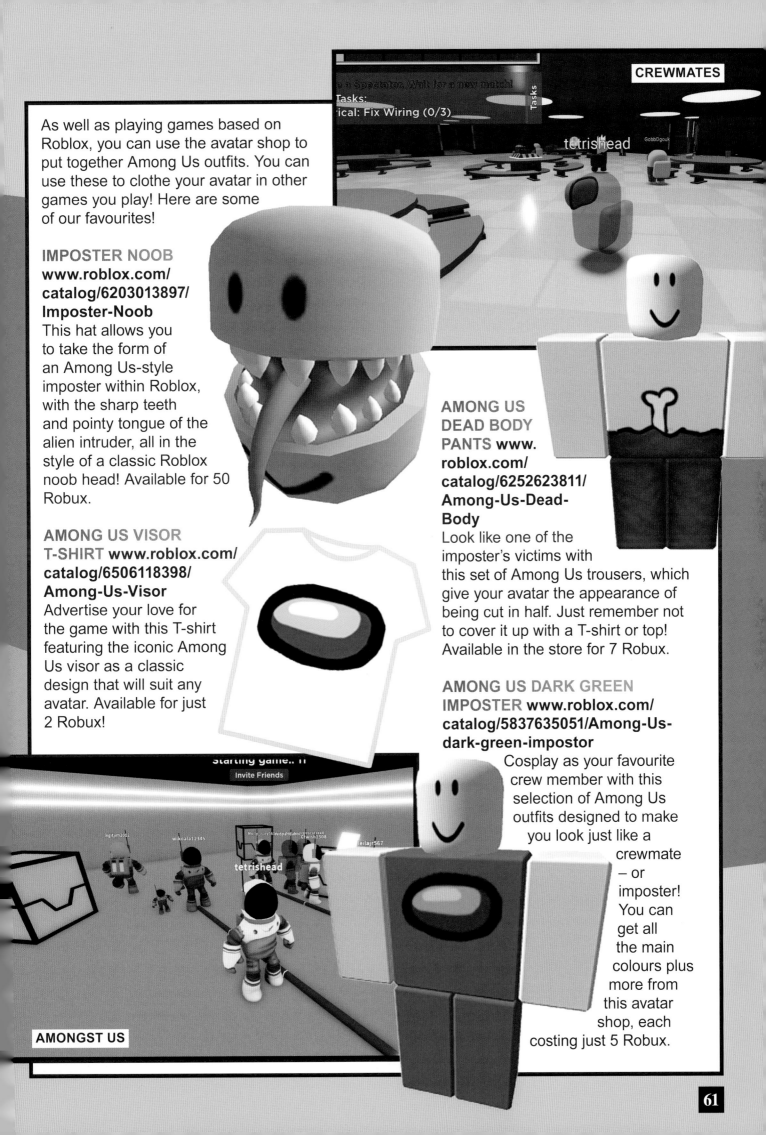

GHOSTED:
WHAT TO DO WHEN
YOU DIE

Did you get taken out? Don't despair – your game isn't over yet!

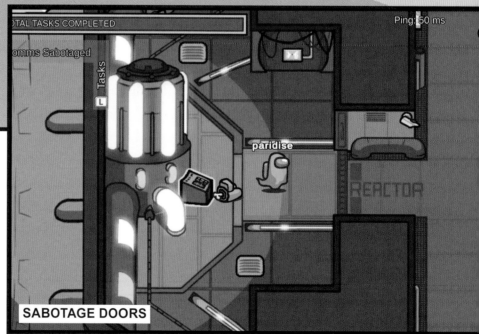

TOTAL TASKS COMPLETED

Ping: 50 ms

omms Sabotaged

Tasks

L

paridise

REACTOR

SABOTAGE DOORS

SABOTAGE DOORS

Ghosts have the ability to stop doors working, and you can use that to a number of advantages. Seal off the imposter to protect the other crewmates. Seal people IN with an imposter, so they're more likely to get killed. Or seal imposters out of a room when you see them approaching! It's great fun to help or hinder either side of the fight!

DRAW CREWMATES IN

The ability to sabotage stuff means you can drive your (living) crewmates to certain areas of the map by causing an issue they need to fix. Whether you do that to make them run past the imposter's hiding place or to get them to leave the area where they're vulnerable is up to you – it's just one option you have when you're a ghost!

SPY ON THE IMPOSTER

It won't be a lot of use in this game, but following the person who killed you will let you learn their secrets. Where they like to hide, how they pretend to be a crewmate, and how they deliver their best kills. You'll learn some tricks, and if you face them in another round you'll know how they operate.

SPY ON THE IMPOSTER

PLAN YOUR NEXT GAME

doesn't make much difference whether you complete them or not, it's a relatively fun way to kill time and get some practice with the tasks available. That way, you'll be able to do them more quickly and efficiently next time!

GO GET A DRINK AND A SNACK!

Sometimes it's hard to tear yourself away from Among Us, so if you die early on, it's always worth grabbing a bit of food and a drink so you can replenish your energy. Take in the game while you eat, then you'll be ready to keep going for another bunch of rounds. Who knows when you'll have this much time free again?

PLAN YOUR NEXT GAME

Everyone in the ghost chat has one thing in common: you all got killed. Clearly, you could have planned some things better! Why not use the time in the ghost chat to plan what you're going to do in the next game to avoid this situation happening again? If nothing else, it will give you time to have a chat with some of your fellow crewmates, so you can learn things that might be handy in the next round.

COMPLETE YOUR TASKS

Ghosts still have tasks to do, and while it

Task Completed!

COMPLETE YOUR TASKS

SETTING UP A
MULTIPLAYER
GAME

Half the fun of Among Us is playing with friends. Here's how to do it

MULTIPLAYER TYPES

There are two types of multiplayer game – local and online. Local refers to several people playing on the same network – if you're all in the same house, connected to the same wifi, for instance – while online refers to playing other people over the internet. Online games can be played against random players, can include your friends, or be made up of groups of ONLY your friends! Here's how to set up all types of game.

LOCAL

To play a local game, click the "local" button to get to the options screen. Here, you'll either see a list of existing games being hosted on your local network or have the opportunity to create one that others can join. This is all fairly simple! Local games are great if you have a lot of people in one place. The fact that the conversations about who's an imposter and who isn't can happen in person means the fun is intense and often hilarious. This is the best way to play the game, if you can! Just make sure your friends can't easily see your screen!

ONLINE

To get into an online game, things are a little more complicated, but not too much! If you click "online", you'll be given a few options: HOST to start an

online game, PUBLIC to find an existing game accepting players, and PRIVATE to join a specific existing game using a code. Additionally (depending on the platform), you may be able to switch your multiplayer region between North America, Europe and Asia. You only need to do that if you want to play against other players, though beware that the lag might increase if you change out of your home region!

HOSTING

Select CREATE GAME, and you'll be placed in charge of setting up a round of Among Us. You'll have a choice of each of the four maps – The Skeld, Mira HQ, Polus and the Airship. You'll be able to select whether the game has one, two or three imposters and the maximum number of players, from four to 15.

Note that the minimum number of players is capped at seven if you have two imposters, and nine if you have three! You'll also be able to select the chat language – leave it as "other" unless you want to restrict yourself to playing in a specific language. Once you've filled these out, hit "create game".

Recommended Settings
Map: The Skeld
Impostors: 1 (Limit: 0)
Confirm Ejects: On
Emergency Meetings: 1
Anonymous Votes: Off
Emergency Cooldown: 0s
Discussion Time: 15s
Voting Time: 120s
Player Speed: 1x
Crewmate Vision: 1x
Impostor Vision: 1.5x
Kill Cooldown: 45s
Kill Distance: Medium
Task Bar Updates: Always
Visual Tasks: On
Common Tasks: 1
Long Tasks: 1
Short Tasks: 2

Ping: 50 ms

paridise

START

HOSTING

CUSTOMIZE

PUBLIC GAMES

When joining a public game, you're able to filter by map type, the number of imposters and the chat language. A list of games meeting your criteria appear below, showing the host and how many players are already in it. Click on one to enter that game's lobby and wait for the round to start!

PUBLIC GAMES

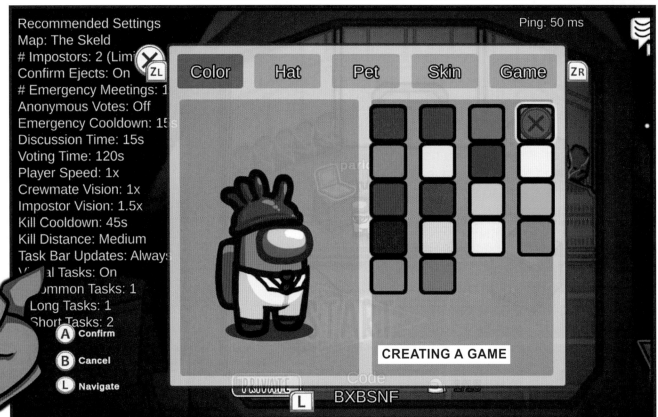

CREATING A GAME

PRIVATE GAMES

To join a private game, simply put in the six-letter code provided by the host and hit the arrow. You'll be taken immediately to that game's lobby.

CREATING A GAME

Whether you're setting up an online game or a local game, you can tweak your options beforehand. If you're playing online, you'll be able to switch your game between private and public (private is the default). You'll also see the six-letter code that allows people to join your game if it's private.

You'll begin in the lobby with a list of the round's specific settings on the left. Other players will join and be able to converse with you while you set up the round. Click on the laptop in the lobby, and you'll be able to set up the look of your player, including choosing a colour, setting a hat, a pet and/or any other

skin accessory. However, the fun part is the game settings…

GAME OPTIONS

If you don't wish to tweak these, you can check "recommended settings" to play using the default ones. However, if you want to change the game, here's what you can do:

IMPOSTERS – change the number of imposters per round after initial setup.

CONFIRM EJECTS – Are you told whether the player ejected was an imposter or not?

EMERGENCY MEETINGS – How many emergency meetings can be called per round?

EMERGENCY COOLDOWN – The minimum length of time between emergency meetings

DISCUSSION TIME – How long, in seconds, do you get to discuss who the imposter is before you can vote?

VOTING TIME – How long do you get to vote? (Discussions can continue during this time)

PLAYER SPEED – How fast characters move

CREWMATE VISION – How far can crewmates see?

IMPOSTER VISION – How far can imposters see?

KILL COOLDOWN – How long must the imposter wait between kills?

KILL DISTANCE – How close imposters must be to kill someone.

VISUAL TASKS – Are visual tasks on or off?

TASK BAR UPDATES – Do you get updates on what actions have been performed?

COMMON / LONG / SHORT TASKS – Three options allow you to choose the number of tasks given to players each round.

PUZZLES

Another test for your Among Us skills!

REWIRE TASK

Here's a challenge for you: can you connect the words below to create tasks you could be asked to perform during a game of Among Us? We've repaired one connection to get you started!

START	DISTRIBUTOR
WATER	SCAN
SUBMIT	GARBAGE
RESET	ENGINE OUTPUT
CALIBRATE	DATA
ALIGN	PLANTS
EMPTY	REACTOR
UPLOAD	BREAKERS

ASSEMBLE	RECORDS
CALIBRATE	SHOWER
DRESS	BURGER
FIX	DISTRIBUTOR
CLEAN	TEMPERATURE
MAKE	ARTIFACT
SORT	TOILET
RECORD	MANNEQUIN

10 TIPS TO WINNING A GAME

Finally, here are a few ideas to give yourself the upper hand in a game of Among Us!

Custom Settings
Map: MIRA HQ
Impostors: 3
Confirm Ejects: On
Emergency Meetings: 3
Anonymous Votes: On
Emergency Cooldown: 15s
Discussion Time: 30s
Voting Time: 30s
Player Speed: 1.75x
Crewmate Vision: 5x
Impostor Vision: 1x
Kill Cooldown: 10s
Kill Distance: Short
Task Bar Updates: Never
Visual Tasks: On
Common Tasks: 2
Long Tasks: 1
Short Tasks: 3

Ping: 76 ms

Bukzu
Funnyjoke
Proudwater
Grayum
Ripeheat
Louvoo
Onerock
Timidcow
Darkstew
Smellfork

STICK TOGETHER   PUBLIC   Code VUWBZF   10/14

1 STICK TOGETHER!

There's safety in numbers in Among Us: if you're alone and a crewmate, you're an easy kill. If you're alone and the impostor, it looks sus!

2 LEARN THE MAPS

Whatever map you're playing on, you give yourself an extra edge if you're already familiar with its layout. If you're struggling, leave the pages of this book open on the guide to the map you're playing.

3 EYES OPEN

What makes Among Us such a challenge is you don't just need to focus on what you're doing; you need to have an idea of what everyone else is up to! Take note of where you see other players, and have a rough idea where they are. It's difficult at the start of a match; it gets a little easier when there are fewer players – but also more dangerous!

4 IF IN DOUBT, CALL A MEETING

It can be annoying when people keep calling meetings, but if you have a good guess as to who the impostor is, you need to call one straight away. The longer you leave it, the riskier it is!

5 REPORT KILLS

If you're a crewmate and you see a body, you need to report that straight away. However, if you're the impostor, why not report it too? You never know, it might just make someone less sus of you!

6 KNOW YOUR COOLDOWNS

Functions in Among Us have a cooldown time attached, and you need to be wary of that. What's more, if you're hiding in a vent, the cooldown clock is paused!

REPORT KILLS

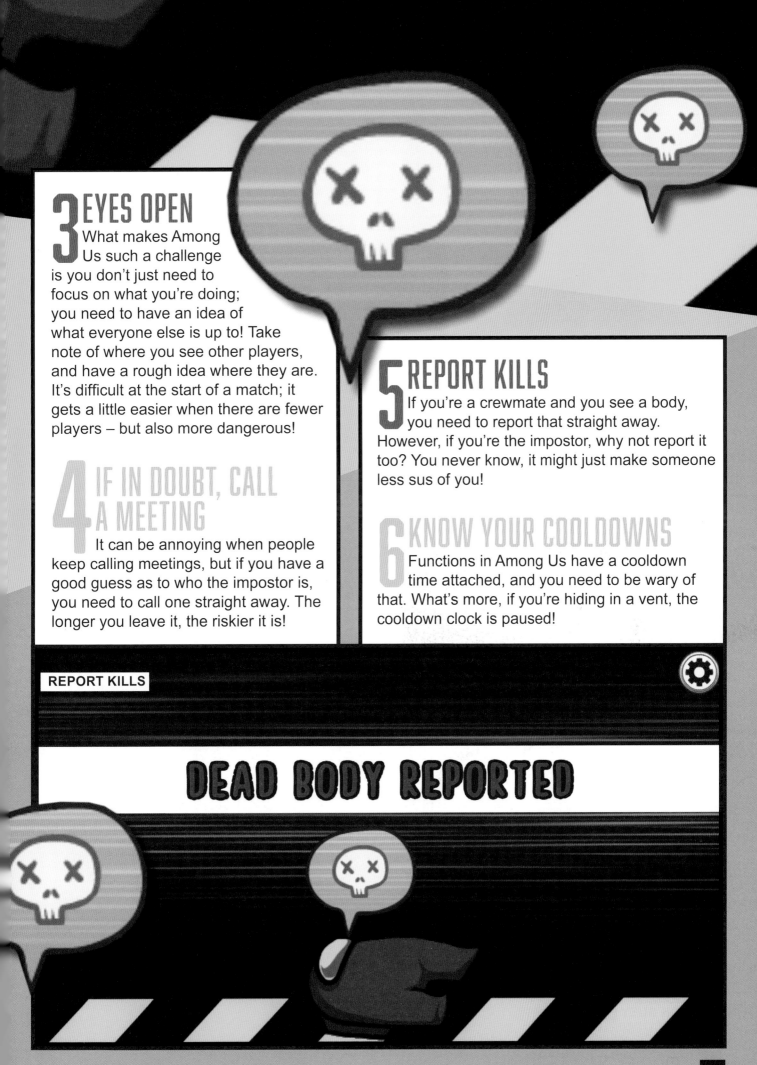

DEAD BODY REPORTED

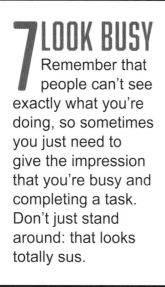

7 LOOK BUSY

Remember that people can't see exactly what you're doing, so sometimes you just need to give the impression that you're busy and completing a task. Don't just stand around: that looks totally sus.

8 WATCH FOR THE RED LIGHT

Don't forget that if you see a red light blinking on a camera, somebody out there is watching! You need to change your actions accordingly.

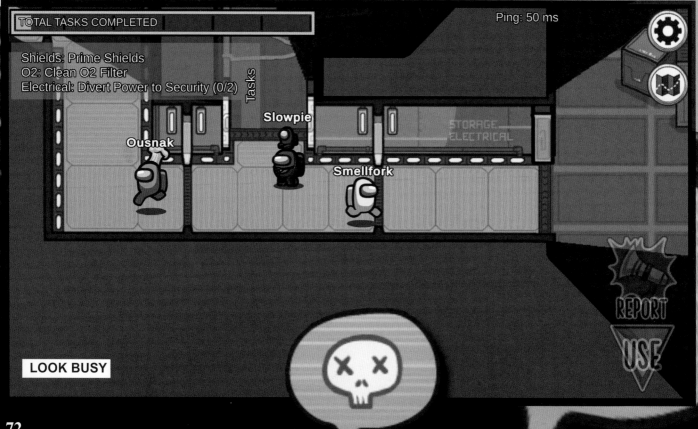

LOOK BUSY

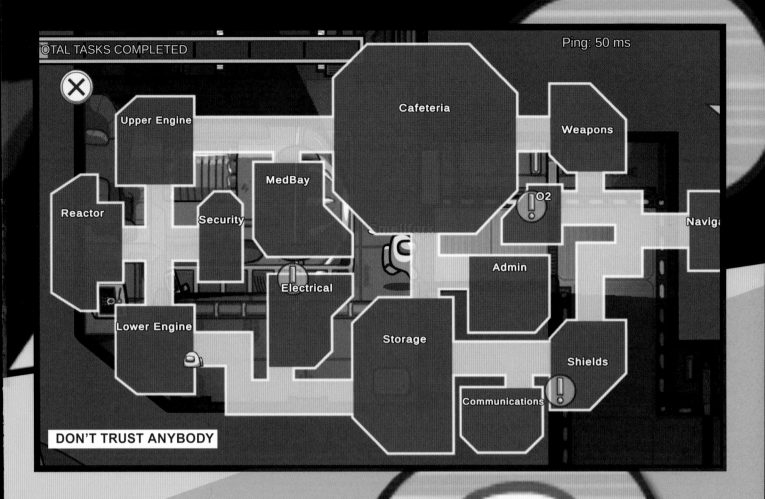

Ping: 50 ms

Cafeteria

Upper Engine

Weapons

MedBay

Reactor

Security

O2

Naviga

Electrical

Admin

Lower Engine

Storage

Shields

Communications

DON'T TRUST ANYBODY

9 FOLLOW THE SABOTAGE!

If there's a sabotage action – particularly a kill sabotage – people will notice who doesn't run to try and sort it out as much as those who do. Why wouldn't you, for instance, want to be seen going to fix the oxygen – unless you were the impostor!

10 DON'T TRUST ANYBODY!

Unless you're sat next to somebody and know for sure that they're crewmate or impostor, you have to assume the worst! Just because someone looks like they're doing a task, for instance, it doesn't mean they're actually doing one. It pays to be suspicious!

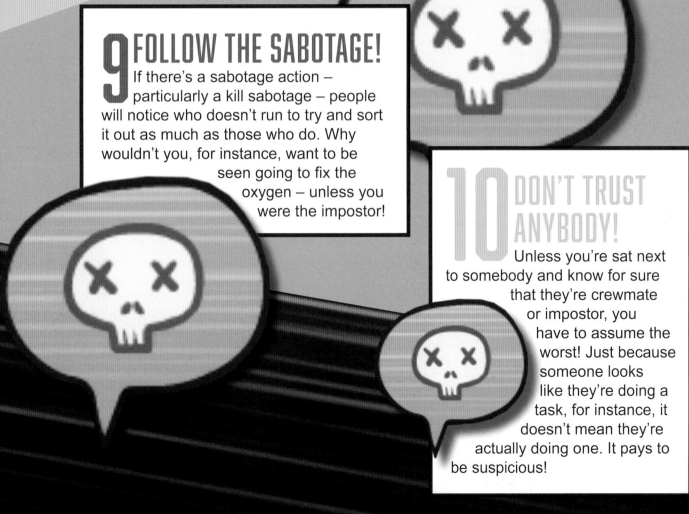

ANSWERS

How well did you do? Find all the answers below!

p20-21: Puzzle 1

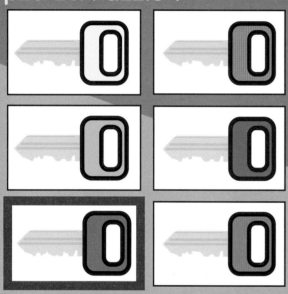

p20-21: Puzzle 2

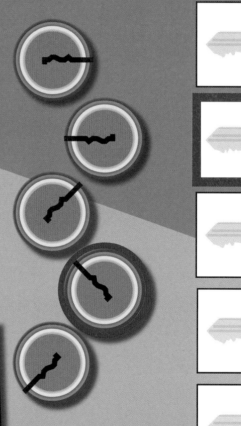

p50-51: Puzzle1

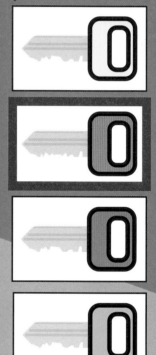

p32-33

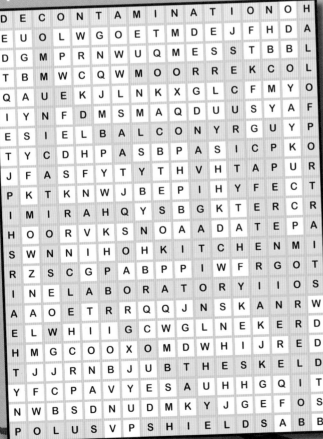

```
D E C O N T A M I N A T I O N O H
E U O L W G O E T M D E J F H D A
D G M P R N W U Q M E S S T B B L
T B M W C Q W M O O R R E K C O L
Q A U E K J L N K X G L C F M Y O
I Y N F D M S M A Q D U U S Y A F
E S I E L B A L C O N Y R G U Y P
T Y C D H P A S B P A S I C P K O
J F A S F Y T Y T H V H T A P U R
P K T K N W J B E P I H Y F E C T
I M I R A H Q Y S B G K T E R C R
H O O R V K S N O A A D A T E P A
S W N N I H O H K I T C H E N M I
R Z S C G P A B P P I W F R G O T
I N E L A B O R A T O R Y I I O S
A A O E T R R Q Q J N S K A N R W
E L W H I I G C W G L N E K E R D
H M G C O O X O M D W H I J R E D
T J J R N B J U B T H E S K E L D
Y F C P A V V Y E S A U H H G Q I T
N W B S D N U D M K Y J G E F O S
P O L U S V P S H I E L D S A B B
```

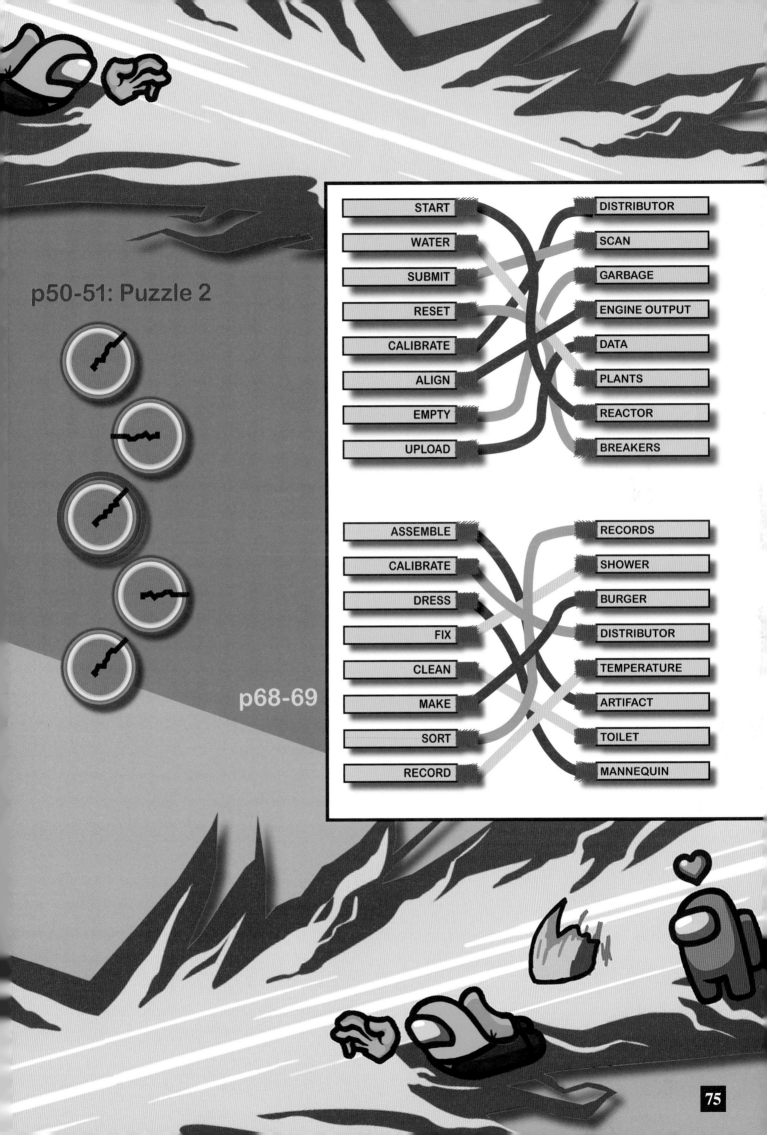

p50-51: Puzzle 2

p68-69

START — DISTRIBUTOR
WATER — SCAN
SUBMIT — GARBAGE
RESET — ENGINE OUTPUT
CALIBRATE — DATA
ALIGN — PLANTS
EMPTY — REACTOR
UPLOAD — BREAKERS

ASSEMBLE — RECORDS
CALIBRATE — SHOWER
DRESS — BURGER
FIX — DISTRIBUTOR
CLEAN — TEMPERATURE
MAKE — ARTIFACT
SORT — TOILET
RECORD — MANNEQUIN

STAYING SAFE ONLINE

Learn how to stay safe online and protect yourself while gaming

BE CAREFUL WHEN PLAYING PUBLIC GAMES

So long as you know all of the players taking part, joining a privately hosted game of Among Us is the safest way to play online. Anyone involved will have been sent a specific code, whereas games set as public can be found and joined by anyone. Public games will inevitably put players in contact with many strangers and that's something to be wary of.

DON'T SHARE THE CODE WITH STRANGERS

If you've been given a code to join a private game, don't share it with anyone you don't know. Why have strangers involved in your game when you're having fun with friends?

USE QUICK CHAT TO COMMUNICATE

The safest way to communicate within Among Us is with Quick Chat. This restricts conversations to pre-selected messages and reduces the chance of being encouraged to give away personal information. If free-text chat is enabled, bad language is removed but some words can slip through, particularly if written to avoid being filtered.

TRY TO STEER AWAY FROM DISCORD

A lot of Among Us players use a third-party voice chat app such as Discord, and the game makers have no control over this. As such, only use these apps with people you know, but try to keep all communication within the game. It's a good idea to allow the sound to come out of the speakers so others can hear anything inappropriate too.

that you are aware of what is good and bad behaviour. Don't be afraid to remove bullies or anyone acting inappropriately. All players must be respectful of one another.

WATCH OUT FOR IN-APP PURCHASES

Players can pay to personalise avatars and remove adverts, but always ask the bill payer's permission before you add money to their credit or debit card. In-app purchases can be turned off on iOS and Android devices. For iOS, tap Settings > Screen Time > Content & Privacy Restrictions, selecting the Content & Privacy Restrictions button before tapping iTunes & App Store Purchases > In-app Purchases > Don't Allow. In Android, head to the Google Play Store, tap the three-line icon and tap Settings > Require Authentication for Purchase. Select For All Purchases Through Google Play On This Device or Every 30 Minutes and confirm using your password.

PLAY TOGETHER

Play the game with your parent or guardian? That way, you can show them how amazing Among Us is and allow them to understand the game better. They'll likely love it too!

SHARE ANY CONCERNS IN REAL LIFE

If you come across anything in the game that makes you feel uncomfortable, tell someone you trust about it. Don't keep it to yourself. If something feels even a little bit wrong, then it's always best to let someone know. It never hurts to be on the safe side.

REGISTER FOR THE PARENT PORTAL

Parents or guardians must give their permission to allow children under the age of 13 to play Among Us. It's then possible to set permissions regarding the use of personal information as well as the features that can and cannot be used, such as free chat. A child's profile can be reviewed, and parents or guardians have control over any changes to the display name.

BE AWARE THAT PLAYERS WILL LIE ABOUT THEIR AGE

Part of the game is to lie and manipulate, so it's perhaps ironic that this can extend to the game as a whole. It's not that difficult for players to give a false birth year, allowing them to get around the restrictions on child accounts. This means parents and guardians should be vigilant about the apps being downloaded to mobile phones, tablets and computers.

BE A GOOD HOST

If you fancy hosting a game on Among Us, it's important